The
401(k)

Anthony J. Domino, Jr.,
CLU, ChFC, MSFS

Howard Rosenfeld,
MAAA, MSPA,
Enrolled Actuary

ADVISOR

Foreword by Andrew J. Fair, Esq.

ISBN: 0-87218-670-9

Library of Congress Control Number: 2005928300

1st Edition

Printed in U. S. A.

Dedications

Anthony J. Domino, Jr.

I would like to thank my wife Meg, as well as my wonderful children, for the love and support to allow me the time to develop the expertise in my field that was required to complete this volume. In addition, I would like to thank Henry Deppe, George Denton and my father, Anthony Domino, Sr., for introducing me to the greatest business and the most wonderful opportunities in the world.

Howard Rosenfeld

I would like to thank my wife Jerri and my children for their love and support during this period. I would also like to thank my office staff for their help, especially my partner, Linda Tortu, for her input and proof reading assistance. Finally, I would like to thank my late father, Aaron Rosenfeld for giving me the insight and the ability to pursue the knowledge it took to produce this volume.

About the Authors

Anthony J. Domino, Jr.

 Anthony J. Domino, Jr., CLU, ChFC, MSFS is the President of Associated Benefit Consultants, LLC. Associated Benefit Consultants is an employee benefit-consulting firm headquartered in White Plains, New York. Through a custom blend of in-house and outside support services, they provide clientele with pension, profit sharing, deferred compensation, employee benefits, as well as financial and estate planning. As such he is also a founding principal of the National Advisors Private Client Group network.

A graduate of Brown University, he is a Chartered Financial Consultant and has earned his Masters in Financial Services. Anthony's specialty is the planning problems facing family owned businesses. Focused attention is given to the transfer of ownership from one generation to the next.

Anthony is President of the Society of Financial Service Professionals, a 22,000-member organization serving accredited professionals. He has served on the AALU Qualified Plans Committee and 2001 Nominating Committee. In 1988 he was honored by The Guardian Insurance Company as New Associate of the Year for his leading production. He has consistently qualified for the Million-Dollar Round Table since entering the business. He has qualified for Top of the Table eight times.

Anthony is currently a member of Guardian's Product Development Council and a Senior Sales Consultant to their Executive Committee, where he has direct input on future products offered by one of the country's top rated insurers.

Anthony, his wife, Meg, and their four children live in Connecticut.

Howard Rosenfeld

Howard Rosenfeld, MAAA, MSPA, Enrolled Acturay, is currently President and Principal Owner of Rosenfeld/Tortu Retirement Planning Co., Inc. located in White Plains, New York. Mr. Rosenfeld has served on the government affairs committee and the conference committee of the American Society of Pension Professionals and Actuaries (ASPPA). He has also has chaired both regional and national meetings for ASPPA and published articles in the *Pension Actuary, Trust & Investments* and *CPA Journal.*

Mr. Rosenfeld has testified on behalf of ASPPA in front of Department of Treasury officials on funding issues related to defined benefit plans and has had several meetings with congressional staffers regarding pension legislation. He is a frequent speaker on pension topics including plan design, funding issues and tax law changes that impact the private pension system.

Mr. Rosenfeld has appeared as a guest speaker for the Foundation for Accounting Education, and the Financial Planning Association of New York. He has also been an annual speaker at the enrolled actuaries meeting since 1998. Mr. Rosenfeld is a member of the American Academy of Actuaries, the American Society of Pension Actuaries and is an Enrolled Actuary.

Foreword

As a frequent speaker on subjects relating to retirement planning, I am often asked by my audience to recommend reading material. I have found it difficult to do so, in part because much of the available information is either too technical to follow, is presented in much too simplistic a fashion to be truly educational, or is written by academics rather than individuals with hands-on experience with the subject.

Anthony Domino and Howard Rosenfeld have that hands-on experience, both in the marketing and design of qualified retirement plans, and in the administration of such plans. That experience makes their book on 401(k) plans a useful tool for anyone interested in the technical and practical aspects of this type of employee benefit program.

I have worked with both Anthony and Howard during the course of my practice as a benefits attorney, and share a number of clients with them. Their experience with 401(k) plans and planning extends from the small sole proprietor plan to large plans benefiting thousands of employees, and they have demonstrated a consistent professionalism in their practices, while at the same time maintaining a practical understanding of the planning required to accomplish the goals of their clients. That professionalism and understanding infuse their book, *The 401(k) Advisor*, with a quality lacking in most books dealing with qualified plans.

The 401(k) plan has become the most popular form of qualified plan. Funds held in such programs are an important part of the retirement income security for many individuals. While investment advice is readily available for most participants and plan sponsors, there is much less clear information available on the design and operation of such plans, despite the fact that operational and administrative concerns are just as important to the success of a 401(k) plan.

The rules governing qualified plans in general, and 401(k) plans in particular, are complex. Both the Internal Revenue Service and Department of Labor conduct continual oversight with reference to plan operation and administration. An understanding of those rules, and their practical application, is essential for those involved with the 401(k) plan.

Anthony and Howard both provide consulting services to employers sponsoring 401(k) plans and employees participating in those plans. They have elected to share the information they possess, together with their practical experience, in the form of this book. The book is written using numerous examples and, by using such examples, Anthony and Howard provide the clearest explanation possible of the 401(k) plan.

With the publication of this book, I now have a recommendation I can make to those looking for a thorough and practical guide to the 401(k) plan.

Andrew J. Fair, Esq.
White Plains, New York

Table of Contents

Chapter 1

401(k) Basics — As Easy as ABC

The last twenty years have seen one of the most dramatic shifts in the history of the American employee benefit marketplace. The revolution associated with the explosion in popularity of 401(k) plans has had a dramatic effect on not only the American workforce, but also the domestic stock market and the basic fabric of our society.

It is difficult to state exactly when the trend caught on, but Section 401(k) of the Internal Revenue Code was added in 1978 (Tax Revenue Act of 1978, P.L. 95-600). As the legislation was signed into law, defined benefit programs were the primary type of retirement plan offered by most employers. Only four years after the groundbreaking reform of ERISA, this sleepy little provision of the Code, nestled between 401(j) and 401(l), would have repercussions a quarter century down the road.

At that time, the landscape was quite different. A total of 128,401 defined benefit plans filed a 5500 tax return in 1978.[1]

The defined benefit was consistent with the mood of the day. Employees tended to work for a single employer for most of if not their entire career. Cradle to grave benefits were far more common. An employer offered full health care coverage at no cost to the employee. Defined benefit plans replaced a set percentage of pay at normal retirement age, which was defined as age 65 for virtually all Americans.[2]

At that time, defined contribution plans were still the primary type of plan (314,592 in 1978)[3], but twenty five years later, all that would change. In 2003 there were 26,000 defined benefit plans and 840,301 defined contribution plans.[4] For the historical elective deferral limits from 1986-2006, see Appendix A.

OK - 401(k) - But What is It?

In its most basic form, a 401(k) plan is simply an employee contributory retirement plan. Contributions are totally discretionary, made on the part of the employee. Each participant determines how much he or she wishes to contribute to the plan, typically expressed as a percentage of pay. Technically, these deposits are called elective deferrals, as each eligible participant has a choice to either receive the amount indicated as current compensation or "defer" receiving this income and the income tax associated with it.

Although employers may make additional deposits, either in the form of a profit sharing or a discretionary formula, which matches employee deferrals, they are not required to do so.

The advantages of saving through a 401(k) plan are significant for the participant. Any deferrals made into the program are accomplished on a pre-tax basis. This, for those who are planning on saving for retirement, the 401(k) is considered the best long-term savings vehicle.

Example 1: Employee A has an annual gross salary of $40,000, is in a 25% tax bracket (effective rate combined federal, state and local income tax rate) and makes an elective deferral contribution to his employer's sponsored 401(k) plan equal to $4,000 (i.e. 10% of his gross salary). Employee B also has a gross annual salary of $40,000, is in the same tax bracket as Employee B, does not contribute to the 401(k) plan and saves the same $4,000 in a personal savings account. Listed below is a summary of the difference in available net income for employees A and B:

	Employee A	Employee B
Gross Salary:	$40,000	$ 40,000
401(k) Savings:	$ 4,000	$0
Income Subject to Tax:	$36,000	$ 40,000
Income Tax:	$ 9,000	$ 10,000
Personal Savings (after tax):	$0	$ 4,000
Net Spendable Income:	$27,000	$26,000
401(k) Advantage:	$ 1,000	

In its simplest form, the 401(k) is the most tax-advantaged method of tax-deferred savings available to the American worker. It stands to reason that for average Americans in a 22% tax bracket,[5] the tax deferred compounding of their deferrals will enhance their balances by almost 30%. Twenty-two percent of tax savings will be invested on a further tax deferred basis. The compounding will increase the balance further. Investment rates and tax brackets staying constant, the overall advantage will grow to roughly 30%. This is before any employer match or contribution is added in.

Notwithstanding the above, many potential participants become confused about the differences between long-term and short-term savings programs. The 401(k) is not a good place to save money that will be used to go on a vacation or buy a new car. Nonetheless, recent changes in the law *have* liberalized the regulations, potentially allowing a participant to take certain hardship distributions for education or the purchase of a first home.

There are also advantages to the employer of sponsoring a 401(k) plan. These advantages come in the form of potential tax savings as well as softer quality of life issues. The owners of a small employer whose employees make deferrals are often allowed to make their own deferrals. In addition, a 401(k) with a healthy level of employee deferrals may actually save an employer funds on subsequent retirement plan deposits. More on testing and employer tax incentives later, as this is the area of complication that most often trips up the uninitiated 401(k) sponsor.

There are distinct environmental advantages that also inure to the employer who has opted to sponsor a 401(k) plan. As mentioned, this program has gained incredible popularity among the American workplace. Virtually half of all defined contribution plans have a 401(k) element contained in them.[6]

The 401(k) has become a recruiting tool for many employers. Once added to the arsenal of employee benefits offered, it can become an inducement to the potential hire. Oddly enough, many employees have become so engrossed in the availability of a 401(k) that they lose sight of the fact that the plan might not even involve financial participation by the employer. The frenzy for 401(k) has become that great.

Plan Limits

Something so good could not be unlimited, even in the world of a kinder and gentler IRS. Section 401(k) is deemed to be so good that the tax code limits how much one person can defer. The 401(k) is essentially a defined contribution plan. As such, the limits are expressed as the lesser of a percentage of pay or a flat dollar amount.

The Economic Growth and Tax Relief Reconciliation Act of 2001 (EGTRRA) created a scenario whereby the individual percentage of pay limit was increased from 25% of pay to 100% of pay. This reflects the liberalization of the 401(k) limits (and overall retirement plan limits) that swept through Congress and was signed by President George W. Bush. More on how these changes affected overall retirement plans, but the 401(k) limits were adjusted as follows:

Year	401(k) Deferral Limit
2003	$12,000
2004	$13,000
2005	$14,000
2006	$15,000

Thus, for 2005, the overall individual annual elective deferral contribution limit is the lesser of 100% of pay or $14,000. For participants who will be 50 or older during the plan year, an additional catch-up contribution is permitted (see below).

Another significant appeal of 401(k) plans for many employees is the fact that assets may be self-directed. Having emerged from the confusing world of defined benefit, where future benefits are described as a percentage of pay, payable at normal retirement age, the simplicity of a "current account" plan came as a welcome change to many employees.

401(k) As a Current Account Plan

The benefit of this current account approach is that a participant's benefit is always equal to the amount in his or her account at any given point in time. Even when a plan account is not fully vested, the account balance is simply a percentage of the amount listed in the account at that point in time. This has become even more simplified as voice response systems (VRU) and the Internet matured to allow participant access 24/7.

In a defined contribution plan, what you see is what you get. Participants have seen their accounts go up (1990's) and down (2000's) in concert with the ebb and flow of the overall market. A 35 year old can invest in a small cap fund, while a 65 year old can opt for his or her own (likely more conservative) allocation. The rules of basic asset allocation can be applied to these long-term investments.

How to Get it In There

One of the central concepts in how funds flow into a 401(k) plan is that all non-rollover deposits made into the program must be made via payroll deferrals. In other words – personal checks or contributions of cash or money orders (don't laugh – we have seen it all) are not suitable methods of making deposits. Technically, personal employee contributions are called deferrals. As such, they must be deferred or diverted from an employee's payroll.

To determine why this is so critical, it is helpful to review a basic concept of taxation and the flow of dollars. If an employer pays an employee wages, the employer receives a tax deduction, and the employee takes the wages and pays ordinary income tax on them. Should the employer retain the funds and not pay them out, then they become taxable at the employer level. In essence, the contribution of the retirement plan involves a scenario where the employer has released the funds, and therefore is entitled to a tax deduction, while the employee has yet to receive the funds, and is therefore not subject to income tax. In order for this to work, the funds must reside in a third structure, a trust. Specifically, a qualified retirement trust.

Thus, making personal deferrals into the plan via anything but payroll deferrals is problematic. Another reason for this restriction has to do with the annual deferral limitation. As defined above, these maximums apply to the individual participant and are applied per calendar year. In today's mobile employment work force, they must be monitored rather carefully. Each taxpayer has just one 401(k) deferral limit for any calendar year. Thus, if John Dough works for ABC Manufacturing Co., has deferred $8,000 for calendar year 2005, and changes jobs to go work for XYZ Servicing Inc, his remaining deferral limit for 2005 is $6,000. This is one of the few qualified limits that is left up to the individual to monitor. (Clearly XYZ has little or no ability to monitor the deposits made by John at ABC).

Discrimination Testing

These deferrals are subject to a discrimination test in the event that there are highly compensated people in the plan. Currently, a highly compensated employee (HCE) is defined as anyone who:

- earned more than $90,000 ($95,000 in 2005, as indexed for inflation) in the prior plan year, or

- was a 5% owner in the current or prior plan year. For this purpose the family attribution rules (as defined under Section 318 of the Internal Revenue Code) apply. Therefore the spouse's, and lineal ascendants and descendants of 5% owners are also considered HCE's, regardless of their income levels.

Conversely, a non-highly compensated employee (NHCE) is defined as anyone, for a particular plan year who is not a highly compensated employee.

In order to prevent employers from establishing deferral only retirement plans and simply deferring the maximum for themselves, the Internal Revenue Code provides for the deferrals to be subject to a discrimination test. Thus, in any given year, the amount that HCEs may actually defer into a 401(k) plan may be limited by the amount that NHCEs actually defer.

In general, most of what happens in the 401(k) world is boiled down to a percentage of pay. These percentages are then compared as relative amounts based upon the average within each category. Thus, if NHCEs have deferred an average of 4% of their pay, the HCEs must defer, on average, no more than 6% of pay. These technical aspects, as well as some exceptions to them, are explained in Chapter 4.

Making Up for Lost Time

There is a unique twist to the 401(k) limits that was added by EGTRRA 2001. As a continuing effort to encourage those closer to retirement to save as much as possible and adjust for the fact that they did not benefit from the increased deferral limits (the deferral limit prior to EGTRRA was $10,500), a catch-up provision was made available. Subject to no testing whatsoever (other than a minimum salary level at least as great as the catch-up contribution amount, as well as categorizing contributions that are required to be part of the 401(k) discrimination test), the catch-up may be made by any individual who has reached age 50 by December 31st of the current year.

Catch-up contributions, much like the salary deferrals themselves, are subject to overall limitations. Graded in over time, these limits may be added to the 401(k) annual limit, as follows:

Year	Catch-Up Limit	401(k) Deferral Limit	Overall limit
2003	$2,000	$12,000	$14,000
2004	$3,000	$13,000	$16,000
2005	$4,000	$14,000	$18,000
2006	$5,000	$15,000	$20,000

As mentioned, there is no testing on the catch-up limit. Thus, assuming all discrimination tests are otherwise passed, the maximum allowable deferral in 2006 will be $20,000 per person.

Chapter Endnotes

1. Employee Benefit Research Institute – *Historical Statistics* – www.ebri.org.

2. No longer simply age 65, normal retirement age is usually based on full Social Security retirement age, which is based upon the actual year of birth. 1937 or earlier is still age 65 . For 1938-1955, it is age 66 and for 1955 and later, it is age 67.

3. See footnote 1.

4. Ibid – figures are for privately trusteed (non-public) entities

5. The Tax Foundation – April 2004 Special Report *Tax Independence Day*.

6. For reporting year 2003 – there were 840,301 DC plans, of which 424,460 had a 401(k) feature.

Chapter 2

Bound at the Hip — The Profit Sharing Plan

Loosening the Noose

Profit sharing plans (PSPs) are perhaps one of the greatest misnomers in the tax code, since profits are not a requirement for making deposits. In fact, many not for profit organizations utilize a PSP as the primary method to make employer-funded deposits into a qualified retirement plan. This is due to the flexibility of these programs. Typically, the formula contained in the trust document for a PSP simply states that deposits are discretionary on the part of the employer. As such, contributions are not contingent upon profits. A sponsor may have profits and not be mandated to make any contributions, or may actually make a deposit when there are no profits within the sponsoring entity.

Recall that a 401(k) plan is actually a subset of a profit sharing plan. Thus, it is most common to find a 401(k) plan paired with a profit sharing option. This creates incredible convenience as it can be accomplished within a single trust document, one tax filing (Form 5500) and combined benefit statements.

Profit sharing deposits are differentiated from matching contributions in the sense that they are made to either all or a subset of employees, independent of the employee's decision to make elective deferral contributions (this is in contrast to a match, which is made solely to those plan participants actually making salary deferrals). The allocation of contributions is spelled out in the trust document and can be made under a broad variety of arrangements. There is an unlimited number of options as to how a profit sharing contribution can be allocated. These are explained in more detail below, but for now, our focus is on the legislation that made the greatest changes to profit sharing programs since ERISA was passed in 1974.

Deduction Limit and Solo 401(k)

In 2001, the Economic Growth and Tax Relief Reconciliation Act (EGTRRA, or the Act) made several key changes to the deduction limits defined in Internal Revenue Code Section 404. Combining the changes made to the deduction limits with the liberalization of the annual additions limit defined in Section 415(c) provides for some very interesting types of planning opportunities.

Prior to this change, the maximum tax deductible limit for a profit sharing plan (or multiple profit sharing plans) was 15% of eligible compensation. In order for an employer to take advantage of the maximum annual additions limit of 25% of compensation, a second plan had to be added to the profit sharing plan. This second plan was generally either a money purchase plan or a target benefit plan. The Act increased the deductible limit for a profit sharing plan to 25% of eligible compensation, thereby rendering money purchase and target benefit plans unnecessary. (However, there may be certain situations for collectively bargained plans to continue their money purchase plans due to contract obligations.)

The second aspect of liberalizing the tax-deductible limit relates to the treatment of 401(k) elective deferral contributions in the computation of the deducible limit. Prior to EGTRRA, the computation of the maximum deductible limit first required the reduction in eligible payroll by the 401(k) elective contributions. The 401(k) elective deferral contributions were then considered part of the deductible contributions when computing the employer's deductible limit. The following example illustrates this point.

Example 1: Company A has an eligible payroll of $1,000,000. Company A sponsors a 401(k) plan that includes a profit sharing plan component. The 401(k) elective deferral contributions are $100,000. Prior to EGTRRA, the maximum tax deducible profit sharing contribution that could have been made by Company A is $35,000 developed as follows:

Eligible Payroll:	$1,000,000
401(k) Deferral Contributions:	$ 100,000
Adjusted Eligible Payroll:	$ 900,000
15% of Adjusted Eligible Payroll:	$ 135,000
401(k) Deferral Contributions:	$ 100,000
Maximum Profit Sharing Contribution:	$ 35,000

The Act completely did away with the requirement that 401(k) elective deferral contributions be considered in the calculation of the maximum deductible contribution. Therefore, for purposes of determining the maximum tax deductible contribution, neither the adjustment to eligible payroll nor the consideration of the 401(k) elective deferrals limit the employer's ability to make a profit sharing plan contribution. Example 2, below, shows the effect of these changes on the company in Example 1.

> *Example 2:* The facts are the same as in Example 1, however the maximum profit sharing plan contribution is increased from $35,000 to $250,000 as follows:

Eligible Payroll:	$1,000,000
401(k) Deferral Contributions:	$ 100,000
Eligible Payroll:	$1,000,000
25% of Eligible Payroll:	$ 250,000
401(k) Deferral Contributions:	$ 100,000
Maximum Profit Sharing Contribution:	$ 250,000

In addition to the liberalization of the deduction rules as described above, there was also a substantial increase in the individual limit as defined under Section 415 made by EGTRRA. Prior to the EGTRRA, the annual additions limit for an individual participant in a defined contribution plan (or defined contribution plans sponsored by the same employer) was the lesser of:

- 25% of compensation, or

- $30,000 (the dollar limit)

EGTRRA removed the 25% limitation and reset the dollar limit to $40,000, with annual indexing for inflation. The individual limit for 2005 is the lesser of:

- 100% of compensation, or

- $42,000 (the dollar limit, as indexed for 2005)

The combination of the liberalization of the deduction limits and the annual additions limits have paved the way for dramatically increased contributions to defined contribution plans that include a 401(k) component. This can best be illustrated in the example below (which has come to be known as a "Uni-K"or solo 401(k) plan):

Example 3: Company B is a one-person corporation, owned by Mr. B. The individual business owner has W-2 income for 2005 of $112,000. The maximum allocation of $42,000 can be provided to Mr. B as follows:

Eligible Payroll:	$112,000
401(k):	$ 14,000
25% of Eligible Payroll:	$ 28,000
Total Allocation ($14,000 + $28,000):	$ 42,000 (combination of profit sharing plus 401(k))

Example 4: The facts are the same as in Example 3, except that Company B employs Mrs. B. Mrs. B's salary is $14,000 for 2005. The total allocation to Mr. And Mrs. B is $56,000 by providing Mr. B $42,000 as shown above in Example 3, plus a 401(k) elective deferral contribution of $14,000 for Mrs. B.

Section 404(a)(7) defines the maximum tax-deductible limit for the combination of a defined contribution and a defined benefit plan sponsored by the same employer to be the greater of:

• 25% of eligible compensation, or

• the amount necessary to satisfy the minimum funding requirement for the defined benefit plan.

The changes discussed above have also paved the way for a combination of a defined benefit plan with a 401(k) plan with increased contribution potential as shown by the example below.

Example 5: The facts are the same as in Example 1 above, however Company A sponsors a defined benefit plan and a 401(k) plan. The minimum funding requirement to fund the defined benefit plan is $400,000. In addition to the $400,000 that has to be contributed by Company A, there is $100,000 of elective deferral contributions made to the 401(k) plan. There is no prohibition for Company A to contribute the full

$400,000, as well as make the $100,000 of 401(k) elective deferral contributions for the applicable tax period.

Allocation Methods

In general the allocation of contributions in a profit sharing plan cannot "significantly" favor the highly compensated employees (this is covered in the nondiscrimination regulations under Internal Revenue Code Section 401(a)(4)). Defined contribution plans will satisfy the nondiscrimination requirements if the plan provides a uniform allocation formula by meeting one of the safe harbor methods defined below. Alternatively, a plan that does not utilize one of the safe harbor uniform allocation methods must satisfy the general test, also described below.

Uniform Allocation Formula

A uniform allocation formula is a formula that provides each eligible plan participant with either the same percentage of plan year compensation (known as a pro-rata allocation), the same dollar amount *or* the same dollar amount for each unit of service performed by an employee during the plan year. All uniform allocation formulas include the allocation of employer contributions and forfeitures for a given plan year. Allocation of earnings, expenses, gains and losses attributable to an employee's account balance are not taken in to account.

Permitted Disparity (Integration with Social Security)

The tax paid by employers for Social Security benefits is currently 7.65% of gross wages. Of the 7.65%, 1.45% is for Medicare benefits, .5% is for disability benefits and 5.7% is for retirement benefits. The disability and retirement benefit portion is taxed up to the Social Security wage base, which is adjusted each year. For the year 2005, the Social Security wage base is $90,000. Since the tax and ultimately the retirement benefit received from Social Security considers wages only up to the taxable wage base, the system provides a disproportionate share of replacement income to those who make less than the taxable wage base. In exchange for this "inequity" many qualified plans can "recapture this difference or disparity."

The rules for permitted disparity are defined in Internal Revenue Code Section 401(l). Listed below is a summary of the difference in allocation rates that is permitted:

Integration Level	Permitted Disparity
Social Security Taxable Wage Base (SSTWB)	5.7%
More than 80%, but less than 100% of SSTWB	5.4%
More than 20%, but less than 80% of SSTWB	4.3%

In all cases, the integration level must be pro-rated for a short plan year. In addition, the permitted disparity percentages are further limited by the "base percentage." The base percentage is defined as the percentage of compensation a participant will receive as an allocation, prior to applying the integration level. The following examples illustrate this point.

Example 6: Listed below are the salaries for the two employees of Company Z:

Employee 1:	$50,000
Employee 2:	$150,000
Total Payroll:	$200,000

The plan allocation formula will be integrated with Social Security, and the SSTWB for 2005 is $90,000. The company has decided to make a contribution of $8,000. The allocation to Employees 1 and 2 is as follows:

Employee 1:	$1,538.50
Employee 2:	$6,461.50

Note the base allocation percentage is 3.077% (i.e. the portion of compensation up to the integration level of $90,000). In addition to the 3.077% of compensation up to $90,000, Employee 2 receives 3.077% for compensation above the integration level. In this example the maximum permissible disparity is limited below the 5.7%, due to the fact that the total allocation is "relatively small."

Example 7: Assume the same facts as Example 6, except that the total contribution has been increased to $30,000. The allocation of the $30,000 is as follows:

Employee 1:	$6,645
Employee 2:	$23,355

Note both employees receive 13.29% of compensation. In addition Employee 2 receives $3,420 (or 5.7% of $60,000).

Uniform Points

A plan is permitted to have an allocation formula that assigns a point value to age, service and plan compensation. It is optional as to whether both age and service are used, however at least age or service must be used. The allocation of the contribution is then based upon a pro-rata share of each individual participant's points total to the point total for all participants. This method is rarely used; however, it can be useful in certain situations.

New Comparability (the general test)

For employers wanting to stray from the design based safe harbors defined above, a plan can allocate contributions in any "definitely determinable way," provided it satisfies the general test for nondiscrimination. The term "new comparability" is derived from the requirement that allocations be "comparable" between highly compensated employees and non-highly compensated employees in order to satisfy the nondiscrimination rules. The precise testing that needs to be demonstrated in order to satisfy these rules is covered in detail in Chapter 5.

Plan Eligibility Rules

A plan that has a 401(k) component, a matching contribution (Section 401(m)) component and a profit sharing plan component is considered three separate plan structures for purposes of satisfying the minimum coverage requirements. Each of the components can define its own set of eligibility standards and entry dates.

For purposes of plan eligibility, in all cases the minimum age requirement cannot exceed age 21. The minimum service requirement for the 401(k) and 401(m) portion of the plan cannot exceed 1 year. The minimum service requirement for the profit sharing portion of the plan cannot exceed 2 years, however if more than 1-year eligibility is used, special vesting rules will apply as discussed below.

There are two general methods for a plan to define how the service requirements will be satisfied. The plan can use the "hours" method or the "elapsed time" method. Under the hours method a "year of service" is defined as a 12-month period for which a specified number of hours of work is required. The number of hours for this purpose cannot exceed 1000 hours. Under the elapsed time method the number of hours worked is not measured; only the amount of time that has "elapsed" is considered. For example, a plan can define the waiting period as three months. Under this definition an employee will be eligible to participate after three months have elapsed regardless of the number of hours an employee may have worked.

A plan must also define "entry date(s)." Entry dates are the actual dates that employees become eligible to participate under the plan. Any entry date(s) can be chosen regardless of the eligibility period selected, however in no event can an entry date be later than six months after the eligibility period has been satisfied. This point is best illustrated by the following example.

> *Example 8:* Plan W defines the waiting period as one year under the "hours" definition of service, and has a single entry date as the January 1 following completion of the 1-year waiting period. John Smith is hired February 1, 2004 and is told that his entry date will be January 1, 2006 (i.e. the January 1 following completion of 1 year of service). Plan W is in violation of the 6-month rule and must therefore have an alternate entry date definition.

> *Example 9:* Assume the same facts as Example 8, however Plan W is re-drafted to define the entry date as the next January 1 or July 1 following completion of the 1-year waiting period. John Smith will now enter the plan on July 1, 2005 and Plan W is in compliance with the 6-month requirement.

> *Example 10:* Assume the same facts as Example 9, except plan W is re-drafted to define the entry date as the January 1 nearest completion of the 1-year service requirement. John Smith enters the plan on January 1, 2005 and Plan W is in compliance with the 6-month requirement.

Vesting the Benefit

Vesting requirements determine the percentage of the account or portion of the account that terminating employees keep when they terminate employment. Since a plan may have three components (i.e. elective deferrals, matching, and profit sharing) there are separate sets of vesting options that may be applied to each component.

First the elective deferral contributions (i.e. 401(k) salary deferrals) and earnings associated with elective deferral contributions are always 100% vested. Since these contributions are monies that an employee had the choice of receiving as current income, this money and associated earnings belong to the employee whenever the employee might terminate employment.

Matching contributions are contributions made by the employer who sponsors the plan. As a result, the employer is given options as to how these amounts (and the associated earnings) will vest, within certain limits. In general the two types of vesting schedules are known as "cliff" vesting and "graded vesting." Cliff vesting is a schedule that allows 0% vesting to a point and then full (100%) vesting thereafter. Listed below is the most restrictive cliff-vesting schedule that can applied to matching contributions (and associated earnings):

Years of Vesting Service	Vesting Percentage
Less than 3	0%
3 or more	100%

An employer can certainly be more generous and allow for a faster vesting schedule if desired. For example a 2-year cliff is permitted, whereas a 4-year cliff is impermissible.

A graded vesting schedule is a schedule that gradually increases the vesting percentage over time. Listed below is the most restrictive graded vesting schedule:

Years of Vesting Service	Vesting Percentage
Less than 2	0%
2 less than 3	20%
3 less than 4	40%
4 less than 5	60%
5 less than 6	80%
6 or more	100%

An employer can be more generous and allow for a faster vesting schedule if desired. For example a graded schedule that starts vesting after one year as opposed to two years is permissible, whereas a schedule that starts vesting after three years is impermissible. In addition, graded percentages greater than those shown above are permissible, whereas graded percentages less than those shown above (for a select number of years) are impermissible.

Profit sharing contributions (and associated earnings) are subject to the following most restrictive cliff vesting schedule:

Years of Vesting Service	Vesting Percentage
Less than 5	0%
5 or more	100%

Profit sharing contributions (and associated earnings) are subject to the following most restrictive graded vesting schedule:

Years of Vesting Service	Vesting Percentage
Less than 3	0%
3 less than 4	20%
4 less than 5	40%
5 less than 6	60%
6 less than 7	80%
7 or more	100%

Both the cliff vesting and graded vesting schedules for profit sharing plan contributions (and associated earnings) revert back to the matching vesting schedules, if the plan is a top-heavy plan (as defined in Chapter 6). In addition, as referred to above, if the eligibility waiting period for a profit sharing plan contribution is more than one year, the vesting is 100% immediately upon plan entry.

Finally vesting service (like eligibility service) can be defined by either using the "hours method" or the "elapsed time method," with one exception. Vesting service can commence with either an employee's date of employment, or the effective date of the plan (or prior plan, if there was a previous plan that existed and was since terminated). Commencing vesting service with the effective date of the plan could prevent employees from terminating with a "full benefit" for those employers who established a plan after many years of not being able to implement one.

Chapter 3

The Carrot - Matching Contribution Options

As discussed throughout this book, 401(k) plans are subject to a unique non-discrimination test. The objective of the test is to insure that the plan and the tax deferrals provided by the plan do not significantly favor the highly compensated employees (HCEs). In order for a 401(k) plan to be successful, there needs to be a good representation of contributions by non-highly compensated employees (this is not the case for safe harbor plans as discussed in Chapter 5). Many companies will offer a matching contribution for the purpose of motivating the non-highly compensated employees (NHCEs) to make elective salary deferral contributions.

Matching contributions can take many forms. They must be a function of the employee elective contribution (there can also be matching contributions made on after-tax voluntary contributions), but can be capped or related to service as will be illustrated in the examples below. Matching contributions (that are not safe harbor matching contributions) can also be subject to a vesting schedule and a minimum number of hours of service requirement, and can be conditioned on employment status at the end of the plan year.

In order for employees to be motivated by the matching contribution, it should be announced early enough to give the employees ample time to make their elective deferral contribution election (for the year). For example, if an enrollment meeting is conducted in December 2005 and a match is announced at that meeting, the employees can make their deferral election before the first payroll in January 2006.

A match can be presented as a guaranteed rate of return on an employee's investment. For example, if a company offers to match 25 cents for every $1 an employee contributes to the plan, the $1 will be worth $1.25, before any consideration for investment earnings. That is a 25% rate of return before any true investment income is included. That is powerful and can certainly be enhanced by increasing the match formula to 50 cents per $1 or greater.

A plan can be written to provide for a match as stated in the document or there can be a discretionary match. If the match is discretionary, then the plan sponsor loses the ability to communicate it in advance, however the sponsor gains the flexibility of waiting to make the contribution based upon corporate profitability or business performance. If the match language in the plan is discretionary, a resolution stating the match formula and the allocation must be adopted by the plan sponsor prior to the end of the plan year.

The matching contribution is subject to the discrimination test provided in Section 401(m) of the Internal Revenue Code. This is discussed in detail in the Chapter 4.

The examples listed below illustrate some of the options available for making matching contributions:

Example 1: The ABC Co. 401(k) Plan that states the ABC Co. will match 25 cents for every $1 of elective deferral contribution made by an eligible employee. The cost to ABC Co. is an unknown, as the amount of elective deferral contributions that will be made by all eligible employees is unknown. However it can be communicated that the employee's investment of $1 will get at least a 25% rate of return on that investment.

Example 2: Assume the same facts as Example 1, however the matching formula does not recognize elective salary deferral contributions in excess of 6% of an employee's compensation. Under this scenario, the maximum expense to the company is 1.5% of eligible payroll (the 1.5% level would be reached only if all employees who are eligible contribute 6% or more of their compensation). Since there is a cap on the matching formula, the expense to the company is controlled.

Example 3: Assume the same facts as Example 2, however the cap on the matching contribution is set at 4.66% of compensation. How did we arrive at 4.66% of compensation? If the employee average deferral rate is

4.66% (to take full advantage of the company match), the highest average deferral rate for the highly compensated employees (HCEs) would be 6.66% (under the discrimination test). In 2005, the cap on elective deferral contributions is $14,000 and the cap on compensation is $210,000. In order for an HCE who is capped at the compensation limit to put away the maximum of $14,000, the applicable deferral percentage is 6.66%. Hopefully the matching formula motivates the non-highly compensated employee group to average 4.66%.

Example 4: Company HIJ has two divisions A and B. The company will match 50 cents for every $1 of elective deferral contribution for employees of division A and dollar for dollar for all employees of division B. As long as the results of this matching contribution satisfy the discrimination test as provided under Section 401(m), it is permissible to have these two formulas within a single plan.

Example 5: Company DEF has the following matching formula: the company will match 2 cents times the number of years of service with the company for every $1 of elective deferral contribution. An employee with 25 years of service will get a matching contribution of 50 cents for every $1 of elective deferral contribution and an employee with 50 years of service will get $1 for every $1.

Once again, this matching approach is subject to the 401(m) discrimination test.

Example 6: Assume the same facts as Example 5; however, if the employee is not employed on December 31 or works less than 1000 hours in the plan year, the matching contribution for that plan year will not be made for that (those) employee(s).

In this example not only must the plan satisfy the discrimination test under Section 401(m), but the plan must also satisfy the "availability" requirement for the matching contribution as prescribed under Section 410(b) (see Chapter 5). Since the matching contribution is not available to those who are not employed on the last day of the plan year, the ratio of those eligible for the matching contribution must satisfy Section 410(b).

Example 7: From time to time, a firm may wish to make what is known as a profit sharing match. Much like a traditional profit sharing allocation, the decision will be made to allocate a fixed dollar amount as a match. For example, assume $25,000 is allocated as a gross matching deposit. These funds are then allocated, typically on a pro-rata basis to the amount of deferrals made throughout the year. For example, if $250,000 of total deferrals were made through the plan, each employee would receive a match equal to 10 cents per dollar deferred.

Example 8: The landscape of firms sponsoring retirement plans has changed a fair amount over the past few years, and there has been an explosion in the number of hedge fund and investment firms. The management companies who sponsor these programs are often organized as partnerships for tax purposes. This type of employer often has a business model requiring a relatively small number of employees. In addition, most if not all of these folks are highly compensated and/or partners in the firm. Assuming that the some want to allocate the maximum to their account ($42,000) and some prefer to defer nothing, these firms love the "multiple match."

For 2005 the math works perfectly. What this entails is a 200% match. Given the limit of $14,000, a 200% match will provide an additional $28,000 deposit, arriving at a total allocation of $42,000. When flowing partner income through to the Form 1040, the net effect will be that those looking to maximize their deposit will bear the full cost of doing so, whereas those who need all of their disposable income can, in effect, defer nothing. (It should be noted, however, that in the case of a NHCE, the amount of this match that may be counted for purposes of the ADP test is limited. (See Chapter 4.)

Timing

The question often comes up as to when the matching contribution should be made. From the employee's perspective, the sooner a match is made, the better (i.e. every pay period). If the plan has a last day requirement, it is recommended that the match be made at the end of the plan year. This is a timing issue since people who terminate during the year will not be eligible for a matching deposit. Backing out matching deferrals can be messy as earnings on these deposits must be removed as well. In addition, this can be a public relations problem and may well delay the processing of termination packages for those terminated. In all cases the match for a given plan year must be made no later than the due date of the business tax return in order to claim it as a tax deduction.

"Truing Up"

If a matching contribution is made every pay period, an employee changes his or her deferral election percentage during the year and some form of cap (or other formula) is in place, there can be discrepancies between the matching contribution that is actually made and the matching contribution that the plan calls for. An adjustment to correct this discrepancy is known as a "true up." This can best be illustrated by the following example:

Example 9: Company J's 401(k) plan states that the company will match 50 cents for every $1 of elective deferral contribution made by an employee not to exceed 6% of compensation. Matching contributions are made every pay period. The plan allows employees to change their deferral election percentage on the first day of the calendar quarter. Payroll for the company is twice per month (24 pay periods per year).

Jack Jones' gross salary is $60,000 and he elects to contribute 4% of compensation on January 1, 2005. Each pay period Mr. Jones has $100 withheld from his $2,500 gross pay and the company makes a matching contribution of $50. On July 1, Mr. Jones increases his deferral percentage to 10%. The company payroll system implements the 6% cap on the matching contribution each pay period. Listed below is a summary of the matching contributions made for the 2005 plan year:

	Gross Pay	Elective Deferral	Match Contribution
January 1 – June 30:	$30,000	$1,200	$600
July 1– December 31:	$30,000	$3,000	$900
Total:	$60,000	$4,200	$1,500

Each pay period during the first half of the year, the cap of 6% is not an issue, as the elective deferral percentage for Mr. Jones is below 6%. However for the second half of the year, the matching formula of 50 cents for a $1 of elective contributions is limited to $150 of elective deferrals (i.e. $75 per pay period). Therefore the company payroll system limits the matching contribution for the second half of the year is $900 (i.e. $75 for 12 pay periods).

On an annual basis, the total of $4,200 is 7% of the $60,000 of gross income for Mr. Jones. On an annual basis the matching formula produces a matching amount of $1,800 (i.e. 50% of $3,600 or 50% of 6% of compensation). Therefore, the company will make an additional $300 match for Mr. Jones prior to the due date of the company's tax return.

A plan can specify whether the matching contribution will made on an annual or more frequent basis. The differential that occurred in the example above can be dealt with provided there is appropriate plan language and consistent administrative procedures are in place.

Vesting

Covered in greater in Chapter 2, it is should be noted that matching contributions (other than those used to satisfy a safe harbor feature) must be subject to a shorter vesting schedule than other contributions. In addition, eligibility for a match may be different than eligibility to make plan deferrals. In many instances, plans offer immediate entry for purposes of elective deferrals, but participants must wait for one year of employment before qualifying for a matching deposit.

Chapter 4

The Stick — Navigating the ADP Test

As discussed in Chapter 1, 401(k) plans are subject to a unique set of rules in determining whether a plan is discriminating in favor of highly compensated employees (HCE's). Matching contributions and after tax employee contributions (i.e. as defined in IRC Section 401(m)) are also subject to a unique set of rules. This chapter will focus on these rules, the consequences of not satisfying the rules and special circumstances where exceptions apply.

Definition of Highly Compensated Employee

To review, the definition of a HCE for a given plan year is any individual who is either:

- A 5% owner (as determined under the top heavy rules) in the current or prior year, or

- Had more than $95,000 (in 2005, as indexed) of compensation in the prior year, and (if the employer chooses to apply the "top paid group" clause) is a member of the "top paid group."

The family aggregation rules of Code Section 318 apply to the 5% owner portion of the definition.

The *top paid group* election gives employers the potential to limit the number of individuals who are considered a HCE, by limiting the number of individuals considered HCE's to the top 20% of those employees who make more than the threshold amount and ranked among the top 20% in actual compensation order (for this purpose total compensation is considered without regard to plan limitations or statutory limitations that may otherwise apply). Any 5% owner who is not in the top 20% would not be considered in the top paid group. The following example will illustrate this point.

> *Example 1:* Employer J has a total of 50 employees. Of the 50 employees, there are five equal owners, their spouses and 20 others who earned more than $95,000 in 2005. Employer J's plan uses the top paid group election. The 5 owners all had compensation in 2005 in excess of $95,000 and all their spouses had compensation less than $95,000 in 2005. The five owners were the highest paid from the company in 2005. Of the 20 non-owner employees only 4 are considered HCE's for the 2006 plan year. The total number of HCE's for the 2006 plan-year is 14 (i.e. five owners, five spouses and four non-owner employees). Without the top paid group definition in the plan, there would be 30 people considered HCEs for the 2006 plan year (the five owners plus the five owner's spouses plus all 20 others who earned more than $95,000 in 2005).

Depending upon the group it may or may not be advisable to use the top paid group election. This must be reviewed on a case-by-case basis.

Once the determination has been made identifying the HCEs and the non-highly compensated employees (NHCE's), the 401(k) and 401(m) discrimination tests can be performed.

The ADP Test

The HCEs average deferral percentage is dictated by the average deferral percentage of the NHCE's. This test is referred to as the ADP (average deferral percentage) test. The chart below summarizes the corridors defined in the regulations:

If the ADP for the Non-Highly Compensated Employees is:	Then the ADP for the Highly Compensated Employees can be:
0-2%	2 times NHCE average
2%-8%	2 percentage points plus NHCE average
8%+	1.25 times the NHCE average

The same chart applies separately to matching contributions and to employee after tax contributions. The test for matching contributions and/or employee after tax contributions is known as the ACP (average contribution percentage test).

For example, if the ADP (or ACP) for the NHCE's is 0.00%, then the maximum ADP (or ACP) for the HCE's is 0.00%. If the ADP (or ACP) for the NHCE's is 1.50%, then the ADP (or ACP) for the HCE's can be up to 3.00%. If the ADP (or ACP) for the NHCE's is 4.00%, then the ADP (or ACP) for the HCE's can be up to 6.00%. If the ADP (or ACP) for the NHCE's is 10%, the ADP (or ACP) for the HCE's can be up to 12.5%.

The ADP is computed by averaging the actual deferral rates (ADR) for each eligible employee covered by the plan. Simply stated the ADR is a fraction with the numerator equal to the elective deferral contributions for a plan year and the denominator equal to the compensation for the plan year. It is permissible to only recognize compensation from the date an employee is considered a plan participant for this purpose, if the plan so provides. If a plan so provides, elective deferral contributions attributable to compensation paid within 2½ months after the end of the plan year can be considered for the prior plan year. For example, for a calendar year plan, an election to defer compensation paid prior to March 15, 2006 for compensation paid between January 1, 2006 and March 15, 2006 for services rendered in 2005 would be considered a 2005 elective deferral contribution.

In addition to the limits imposed on highly compensated employees by the ADP and ACP tests, the maximum amount that may be deferred each year by any person is defined by Sections 402(g), 414(v) and 415 of the Internal Revenue Code. Section 402(g) sets forth a maximum amount that is subject to cost of living adjustments. Listed below are the Section 402(g) limits through 2006 for traditional and safe harbor 401(k) plans:

Year	Maximum Elective Deferral Limit
2004	$13,000
2005	$14,000
2006	$15,000

Section 414(v) defines the maximum additional elective deferral contribution (known as the "catch-up" contribution) over and above the limits defined by Section 402(g) (or other limits as explained in more detail below). These additional contributions are available only to those employees who attain the age of 50 before the end of the plan year. Listed below are the Section 414(v) limits through 2006 for traditional and safe harbor 401(k) plans:

Year	Maximum Catch-up Contribution
2004	$3,000
2005	$4,000
2006	$5,000

Lower limits apply to SIMPLE 401(k) plans, as explained in Chapter 5. Both the 402(g) and 414(v) limits are calendar year limits applied individually to each participant. Therefore, an individual who changes employers during the year may be limited in making an elective deferral contribution in his or her new employer's plan, if elective deferrals were made in the prior employer's plan.

The catch-up contribution is distinguished from and in addition to "regular" elective deferrals for those who attain the age of 50 before the end of the plan year if any one of the following three circumstances applies:

- The individual has contributed the elective deferral limit defined by Section 402(g),

- The plan sets a cap on elective deferrals in the document,

- There is a failure of the ADP test for the plan year and the "regular" elective deferrals for the plan year are "recharacterized" as catch up contributions.

The following example illustrates this last point.

Example 2: Listed below is a summary of the ADP test for Company DEF's 401(k) plan for 2005 with only one highly compensated employee who is 52 years old:

	Plan Compensation	401(k)	ADP
HCE	$210,000	$10,500	5.0%
NHCE #1	$50,000	$0	0.0%
NHCE #2	$40,000	$2,400	6.0%
NHCE #3	$35,000	$700	2.0%
NHCE #4	$30,000	$0	0.0%
ADP for NHCEs:	2.0%		
ADP for HCE:	5.0%		

The ADP test has failed for 2005, since the maximum permitted ADP for the HCEs is 4.0%. However, if we recharacterize $2,300 of the HCE's contribution from elective deferral money to a catch-up contribution, and the ADP test is redone, this reduces the elective deferral for the HCE to $8,200. The ADP test is now satisfied and no refunds or other adjustments have to be made for the 2005 plan year.

Finally Section 415 does not permit the summation of all annual additions for a "limitation year" to exceed the smaller of:

- 100% of compensation

- $42,000 (in 2005, as indexed, not including the catch up contribution).

For HCEs, elective deferrals that are made for a plan year in excess of the 402(g) limits are taken into account for purposes of the ADP test, whereas they are not taken into account for NHCEs despite the fact that these excess deferrals have to come out of the plan (the timing and penalty taxes that apply are discussed below). Contributions that are designated as catch-up contributions (as described above under Section 414(v)) are not taken into account under the ADP test.

If a plan has only highly compensated employees, the plan is deemed to pass the ADP test under a special exception. In addition, if a plan has only NHCEs the ADP is automatically satisfied.

Plans That Have "Early Participation"

A plan that defines eligibility more leniently than the maximum age (age 21) and service (one year of service) requirements (as defined in Section 410(a)(1)(A)) can determine the ADP test in one of three ways.

- First, the ADP test can be done for the plan as a whole with no recognition of the fact that the plan has more liberal eligibility requirements.

- Next, the ADP for all eligible HCE's for the plan year and the ADP for all eligible NHCE's for the applicable year can be tested separately, disregarding all NHCE's who have not met the minimum age and service requirements (assuming the maximum age and service definition applied to the plan) can be used.

- Finally, the plan may be "disaggregated" into separate plans and the ADP test can be performed separately for each plan. The first plan would be all those employees who completed the minimum age and service requirements and the second plan would be all eligible employees who have not completed the minimum age and service requirements, based upon the maximum age and service requirements that could have been used. Provided each of the "component plans" satisfies the coverage requirements, if each component plan satisfies the ADP test, then the entire plan is deemed to satisfy the ADP test for the plan year.

Current Year/ Prior Year Testing

A plan can use either current year testing or prior year testing for ADP compliance; however, there are restrictions on switching between the two methods. First a definition of these terms:

With prior year testing, the ADP (or ACP) for the NHCEs is calculated using the actual deferral rates (ADR) (or actual contribution rates, ACR) from the plan year *immediately preceding* the plan year for which the ADP test is being performed.

With current year testing, the ADP (or ACP) for the NHCE's is calculated using the ADRs (ACRs) from the *current year* for which the ADP (or ACP) test is being performed.

In either case, the ADP (or ACP) for the eligible HCE's is the average of the ADRs (ACRs) for the HCEs for the plan year for which the ADP (or ACP) test is being performed (i.e. current year results are always used for the HCEs).

The testing method must be defined in the plan document. A plan is always permitted to use the current year testing method; however, if plan wants to be amended to switch from using the current year to the prior year testing method, the current year testing method had to be used for each of the last five years (or less, if the plan has been in existence for a shorter time period). There are special rules for plans that are being tested as a result of a merger or disposition, and the transition rules that may apply.

For a plan's first year, the plan may either use current year results or may compute the ADP (ACP) for the NHCEs or assume 3% as the prior year's ADP (or ACP) for the NHCEs.

A plan may use different testing methods for the elective deferrals than is used for the matching contribution (or after tax employee contribution). For example a plan can use the current year testing method for elective deferrals and the prior year testing method for the matching contribution.

What remains unclear, even after publication of final regulations is the required timing of a plan amendment when a change in testing method is desired. Most practitioners have operated with the notion of amending prior to 2½ months after the end of the plan year, as this is the deadline for making a correction to a failed test if the refund method is selected (as explained below).

What is abundantly clear is that changing testing methods (or making plan amendments) with any sort of frequency that appears to consistently improve the results for the highly compensated employees will violate the purposes of the nondiscrimination rules and could subject the plan to disqualification.

Correction Methods for a Failed Discrimination Test

A discrimination test is failed if the difference between the average deferral or contribution percentages for the highly compensated employees and the non-highly compensated employees falls outside the corridors defined above. When this occurs for a given plan year, a correction must be made in order for the plan to maintain its qualified status.

In broad strokes there are two possible remedies. Either the deferral rates for the highly compensated employees must be reduced via a refund of excess contributions (plus associated earnings) or the deferral rates for the non-highly compensated employees must be increased by some form of employer contribution.

Refund Excess to Highly Compensated Employees

If the refund option is selected, a specific method under the regulations defines how much of a refund needs to be assigned to each highly compensated employee (the adjustment is made on a dollars basis as opposed to a percentage basis, once the average percentages are computed and adjusted). It is possible, depending on the situation, that some HCEs will not receive a refund. The (investment) income portion of the refund can be determined based upon any reasonable method; however, for the period of time from the end of the plan year to the date the refund is made, earnings must also be apportioned. This period is known as the *gap period* and there are several methods defined in the regulations that are acceptable for computing earnings during the gap period.

The refund must be made within 12 months after the end of the plan year. If the distribution is made prior to 2½ months after the end of the plan year the individual must recognize such income for the year in which the deferral was made. This leads to some confusing tax reporting, which will be explained in the example below. If the distribution is made later than 2½ months after the end of the plan year, the individual recognizes the income for the year in which the income was received. In this case the employer is subject to a 10% penalty (excise) tax.

In any case, the distributions that occur as a result of a failed discrimination test are not subject to the 10% excise tax for early distributions nor are they subject to any spousal consent requirements.

Example: Mr. Smith is a highly compensated employee and has been advised that his company's 401(k) has failed the discrimination test for the 2004 plan year (calendar year plan). Mr. Smith received his refund check on March 1, 2005. Despite the fact that Mr. Smith received this distribution in 2005, it must be recognized as 2004 income. Mr. Smith will receive a 2005 Form 1099-R from the plan. This 1099-R will identify with a special code that this income was attributable to the 2004 tax year, and can be delivered to Mr. Smith until January 2006. Therefore, it is important to advise individuals (or their tax preparers) that this awkward method of reporting is in place. If Mr. Smith filed his individual tax return prior to March 1, 2005, he would have to file an amended return.

Refunds of excess contributions are applied against an individual's Section 415 limit (as defined above) and cannot be considered towards satisfying the minimum required distribution rules.

Qualified Non-Elective Contributions and Qualified Matching Contributions

The other method of correcting a failed discrimination test is for the employer to make a nonforfeitable (fully and immediately vested) contribution. This type of contribution can be in form of a qualified non-elective contribution (QNEC) or qualified matching contribution (QMAC).

The timing of making the QNEC and/or QMAC depends upon whether the plan is using the prior year or current year testing method. If the plan uses the prior year testing method the QNEC and/or QMAC must be contributed by the of the plan year being tested. For example, a plan's calendar year 2005 discrimination test based upon prior year testing must make the QNEC and/or QMAC by December 31, 2005. If the plan uses the current year testing method, then the QNEC or QMAC must be made by the end of the subsequent plan year.

The allocation of QNECs and QMACs must also satisfy the general nondiscrimination requirements as defined in regulations under Section 401(a)(4). This is true whether or not the QNECs or QMACs are used in the discrimination test.

In addition, the allocation among the NHCE's is limited to 5% of compensation or two (2) times the "plan's representative contribution rate." This requirement is included in the final 401(k) regulations issued in late 2004, to cure what was deemed as an abuse referred to as "bottom up" QNECs. Prior to this addition, a QNEC of say $100 could have been applied to an NHCE who had only $100 of income for a given plan year, making his or her contribution 100% for ADP test purposes. Effective January 1, 2006, this type of "disproportionate" allocation cannot be used in the ADP test. For this purpose a plan's representative contribution rate is lowest rate for any NHCE among a group of half the eligible NHCEs or any NHCE who is employed on the last day of the plan year, if greater.

Finally, a QNEC and/or QMAC can be is used for only one discrimination test for a single plan year. Therefore if a plan made a QNEC and/or QMAC for the 2005 plan year under the current year testing method and changes in 2006 to the prior year testing method, the 2006 ADP test cannot reflect the 2005 QNEC and/or QMAC.

Correcting a Failed ACP Test

Similar to a failed ADP test, a failed ACP test must be corrected. Making an additional contribution to NHCEs to raise the contribution rates is permissible. This can be done with QNEC's and/or QMACs as described above. These corrections are subject to the same nondiscrimination and disproportionate rules described above for the ADP test.

The differences between a failed ADP test and a failed ACP test are:

- To the extent there is a vesting schedule applied to the matching contribution, a refund to a highly compensated employee will receive only the vested portion of the excess matching contribution (and associated investment earnings). The non-vested portion of the excess matching contribution is a forfeiture. Forfeited matching contributions that are allocated to other participants are counted for purposes of Section 415 for both the individuals receiving an allocation and the individuals who are forfeiting the match.

- Matching contributions are a function of the employee contributions (whether they are pre-tax or after tax employee contributions). Matching contributions associated with excess contributions must comply with the general non-discrimination requirements of Section 401(a)(4). The regulations permit forfeiture of matching contributions that would otherwise cause the plan to fail the general nondiscrimination requirements under Section 401(a)(4).

Chapter 5

Design-Based Safe Harbors

With 1996 legislation, the world of 401(k) plans was given a boost that propelled their popularity even further. The Small Business Jobs Protection Act of 1996 created two new types of 401(k) plans that guaranteed success for any plan sponsor who opted to adopt one: safe harbor plans and SIMPLE 401(k) plans. Prior to 1997, all 401(k) plans were subject to a discrimination test of elective deferral contributions (the actual deferral percentage test—see Chapter 4). Plans with matching contributions were subject to a separate and distinct discrimination test with regard to employer matching contributions. There was also a combined test that sometimes had to be satisfied.

All discrimination tests have the common objective of limiting the contributions made by or for the highly compensated employees as compared to the benefits that are being provided to the nonhighly compensated employees. For plans subject to testing, if the results of the discrimination tests are not within acceptable corridor limits in a particular plan year (see Chapter 4), corrective measures must be taken. The remedies are to either refund contributions to highly compensated employees or make additional contributions for non-highly compensated employees, within specified time frames.

Often these tests were performed long after the participant had either filed his or her own tax return (sealing the exclusion of salary deferrals) or had invested the assets and experienced some type of gain or loss. At a minimum, this corrective process was cumbersome and confusing to the plan participants. All of this may be completely avoided with a design-based safe harbor. There are two such designs available: SIMPLE 401(k) plans (discussed later in this chapter) and the much more popular safe harbor plan.

Safe Harbor Plans

Safe harbor plans became available in 1999, offering employers the potential of freedom from ADP/ACP testing in exchange for meeting special requirements. The "price tag" for receiving safe harbor treatment is an employer contribution to the plan. The employer contribution can be either:

- A 3% nonelective contribution for all eligible employees, or

- A matching contribution using a specific formula (explained below).

In order to qualify as a 401(k) safe harbor plan for a given plan year the following must occur:

1. A notice must be provided to each eligible employee describing the safe harbor contribution. For an existing 401(k) plan, the notice must be provided at least 30 (but not more than 90) days prior to the beginning of each plan year.

2. There cannot be any conditions put on an employee who would otherwise qualify. For example, if a plan has a requirement that an employee has to be employed on the last day of the plan year in order to receive a contribution, that requirement cannot apply to the safe harbor contribution.

3. All safe harbor contributions must be 100% vested at all times.

4. A new 401(k) plan will qualify provided the plan year has been in existence for at least 3 months. Any plan that does not contain a 401(k) provision is considered a new plan for this purpose.

The 3% Safe Harbor Nonelective Contribution

The 3% safe harbor requires a nonelective contribution of 3% of eligible compensation for all plan participants. Since this is *not* a matching contribution it is provided to all eligible employees regardless of their own level of participation. Eligible compensation for this purpose is defined as compensation that is defined by the plan; therefore, compensation is limited by Section 401(a)(17) of the Internal Revenue Code. In addition, if the plan defines compensation "as a participant" and there are multiple (more than one) entry dates within a plan year, compensation for this purpose will reflect only that portion of the year as defined.

The "commitment" to make the 3% safe harbor contribution can be "reversed" provided two conditions are satisfied:

(1) the notice states that the plan may be amended during the plan year to provide a non-elective contribution of at least 3%, and

(2) if the amendment is made, a supplemental notice must be provided at least 30 days prior to the end of the plan year (i.e. December 1 for a calendar year plan).

The 3% safe harbor contribution can be used to satisfy two other requirements that may apply to a plan: the top heavy minimum and the profit sharing contribution required for new comparability testing.

Top-Heavy Minimum

A plan is top-heavy for a given plan year when 60% of the account balances are attributable to key employees as of the last day of the previous plan year. For example if 60% or more of the account balances are attributable to key employees on December 31, 2004, the plan is deemed top-heavy for 2005. If a 401(k) plan is top heavy the plan sponsor is required to make a top-heavy minimum contribution for all non-key employees. The top-heavy minimum contribution is the lesser of:

- 3% of compensation, or

- the highest contribution (including forfeiture) allocation made to any key employee.

The following example will clarify this application of the top-heavy minimum in 401(k) plans.

Example 1: Employer A is the sponsor of 401(k) Plan A that covers 10 non-key employees and 2 owners. The account balances for the two owners as of December 31, 2003 totalled $500,000 and the total plan assets were

$750,000. For the 2004 plan year the plan is top-heavy and the key employees made elective 401(k) contributions of 6% of eligible compensation. Employer A is required to make a 3% top-heavy minimum contribution for the 2004 plan year.

Example 2: Assume the same set of facts as Example 1, however the key employees do not make any contributions to the plan, nor are any employer contributions or forfeitures allocated to the accounts of the key employees. Despite the fact that the plan is top-heavy for 2004, the top-heavy minimum contribution for 2004 is $0.

In most cases the key employees of a top-heavy plan will be receiving allocations that are least equal to 3% of compensation. In these cases the top-heavy minimum of 3% of compensation will apply. Since the top-heavy minimum contribution and the 401(k) safe harbor contribution are the same required deposit of 3% of compensation, adopting a safe harbor provision for a top-heavy 401(k) plan is a logical progression. It is important to note, however, that if the employer adopts a 401(k) safe harbor plan, the 100% vesting requirement as well as the requirement of a contribution for those not employed at the end of the plan year become added "long term" costs.

Profit Sharing Contribution

The 3% safe harbor contribution can also be treated as a profit sharing contribution. This is a helpful plan design technique in that the safe harbor contribution can serve three purposes: as discussed above, (1) the safe harbor contribution can be used to guarantee that the 401(k) discrimination test is satisfied, (2) it can be used as a top-heavy minimum contribution and (3) it can be used as a basis for a profit sharing contribution.

The allocation of a profit sharing contribution is subject to a different (and independent) nondiscrimination test under section 401(a)(4) of the Internal Revenue Code. In order to demonstrate satisfaction of the nondiscrimination requirements, the allocation of a profit sharing contribution can be tested on either a contributions or benefits basis. The regulations under 401(a)(4) provide for design based safe harbor plans whereby all plan participants effectively receive the same allocation expressed as either a level dollar amount or the same percentage of compensation. Alternatively, a plan can be designed outside of the design based safe harbor options, provided the plan can satisfy the general test.

The allocation rates for a plan that is using contribution-based testing are determined by dividing the allocation provided by the plan compensation. These rates can make use of permitted disparity (equivalent to Social Security integration) as provided in the regulations.

The allocation rates for a plan that is using benefits based testing are determined by first converting the allocated contribution to a benefit (i.e. an annuity payable for life) at the plan's testing age. This converted benefit is then divided by plan compensation to derive what is called an "equivalent benefit accrual ratio" (EBAR).

The use of converted benefits to demonstrate satisfaction of the nondiscrimination test for a defined contribution plan, or the use of contributions to demonstrate compliance for a defined benefit plan is known as "cross testing."

The concept behind the general test for nondiscrimination is that each highly compensated employee who receives an allocation under the plan and all other plan participants who receive an allocation that is equal to or greater than the allocation of the particular highly compensated employee being tested, constitute a rate group. Each rate group under the plan must satisfy the coverage requirements as though it were its own separate qualified plan.

Coverage

The coverage requirements are defined in Section 410(b) of the Internal Revenue Code and the regulations thereunder. There are effectively two options under Section 410(b). The first is called the ratio test. The ratio test is satisfied if the result of the following division (Fraction A/Fraction B) is at least 70%:

$$\text{Fraction A} = \frac{\text{\# of Non-Highly Compensated Employees in the rate group}}{\text{Total \# of Non-Highly Compensated Employees}}$$

$$\text{Fraction B} = \frac{\text{\# of Highly Compensated Employees in the rate group}}{\text{Total \# of Highly Compensated Employees}}$$

For both Fraction A and Fraction B the denominator need only consider those employees who have satisfied the age and service requirements.

The following example will illustrate these concepts.

Example 1: Plan W has only one highly compensated employee (HCE#1) and 10 non-highly compensated employees (NHCEs 1-10) who are eligible to receive an allocation. Listed below is the allocation of the profit sharing plan as specified by the plan's allocation formula:

Name	Compensation	Allocation	Allocation Rate
HCE#1	$205,000	$20,500	10%
NHCE #1	$25,000	$ 2,500	10%
NHCE#2	$30,000	$ 3,000	10%
NHCE#3	$35,000	$ 3,500	10%
NHCE#4	$40,000	$ 4,000	10%
NHCE#5	$45,000	$ 4,500	10%
NHCE#6	$50,000	$ 5,000	10%
NHCE#7	$55,000	$ 5,500	10%
NHCE#8	$60,000	$ 3,000	5%
NHCE#9	$65,000	$ 3,250	5%
NHCE#10	$70,000	$ 3,500	5%
Total:	$680,000	$58,250	

The ratio test is satisfied for this plan as follows:

Fraction A:	7/10= 70%
Fraction B:	1/1= 100%
Ratio Test:	Fraction A/Fraction B= 70%

The second method of satisfying the coverage requirements, in lieu of the ratio test, is called the average benefits test. The average benefits test is a 2-pronged test. The first part, called the "classification test" for purposes of Section 401(a)(4) testing, requires the computation of the ratio test for each rate group; however, in lieu of each rate group satisfying the 70% requirement there are lower percentages that are permissible depending upon the plan's concentration ratio. The concentration ratio is simply defined as:

$$\frac{\text{Number of NHCE's (Eligible)}}{\text{Number of HCE's (Eligible)}}$$

The table shown in Figure 5.1 provides the reduced ratio percentages that are permissible for the various concentration percentages.

FIGURE 5.1

Nonhighly compensated employee concentration percentage	Safe harbor percentage	Unsafe harbor percentage	Nonhighly compensated employee concentration percentage	Safe harbor percentage	Unsafe harbor percentage
0-60	50.00	40.00	80	35.00	25.00
61	49.25	39.25	81	34.25	24.25
62	48.50	38.50	82	33.50	23.50
63	47.75	37.75	83	32.75	22.75
64	47.00	37.00	84	32.00	22.00
65	46.25	36.25	85	31.25	21.25
66	45.50	35.50	86	30.50	20.50
67	44.75	34.75	87	29.75	20.00
68	44.00	34.00	88	29.00	20.00
69	43.25	33.25	89	28.25	20.00
70	42.50	32.50	90	27.50	20.00
71	41.75	31.75	91	26.75	20.00
72	41.00	31.00	92	26.00	20.00
73	40.25	30.25	93	25.25	20.00
74	39.50	29.50	94	24.50	20.00
75	38.75	28.75	95	23.75	20.00
76	38.00	28.00	96	23.00	20.00
77	37.25	27.25	97	22.25	20.00
78	36.50	26.50	98	21.50	20.00
79	35.75	25.75	99	20.75	20.00

The second part of the 2-pronged test is called the "average benefits percentage test." The average benefits percentage test requires the computation of each participant's allocation rate (for those plans that are tested on the basis of contributions based tested) or "equivalent benefit accrual ratio" (EBARs—for those plans that are tested on the basis of benefits). An average rate is then developed for all eligible NHCEs and divided by the average rate for all eligible HCEs. The result of this ratio must be at least 70%. Using the average benefits percentage test requires inclusion of all sources of benefits including 401(k) and matching contributions (if applicable). This is in contrast to the ratio test where the only the profit sharing contribution had to be considered.

The combination of cross-testing and utilizing the average benefits test has given rise to the most popular plan design technique that has been employed during the past several years, known as new comparability (explained below). For purposes of this chapter, is important to note that the 3% safe harbor contribution can be used in testing the profit sharing plan contribution as part of a new comparability plan design.

The use of new comparability plans became so widespread that there were proposals by the IRS in 2002 do away with them. However due to extensive lobbying efforts by pension plan professionals and the large number of plans that were created as a result of new comparability plan design, the IRS relented and issued guidance[1] that modified the rules, but allowed the plans to continue to operate.

New Comparability Plan

The term "new comparability" refers to plans that provide unequal allocations to various groups of employees within a particular plan. As explained above, this type of allocation is allowed by the final non-discrimination regulations and the "bright line testing" that is permitted to demonstrate nondiscrimination.

The most popular type of "new comparability" plan is a profit sharing plan (including a profit sharing plan combined with 401(k) and 401(k) safe harbor) where there are various groups within a plan that receive different allocations (as a percentage of compensation). Since the different allocation rates (by their nature) provide different amounts of contributions for different groups of people, the only way such an allocation can satisfy the nondiscrimination requirements is if it is tested on the basis of the benefits it provides (i.e. cross testing).

In order to use cross testing in a new comparability plan the employer contribution is subject to a "minimum gateway requirement". Consider the "minimum gateway requirement" as a toll in order to cross the bridge. Just as paying the toll allows you to cross the bridge, making the minimum gateway requirement contribution allows a plan to use cross testing to demonstrate nondiscrimination, where not all eligible participants receive an *equivalent benefit accrual rate* (EBAR). Of course simply making the minimum gateway contribution does not guarantee that the plan will pass the nondiscrimination test, but it cannot even be considered without this minimum payment. The minimum gateway contribution must be provided to all eligible non-highly compensated employees and must be the lesser of:

- 5% of compensation *or*

- ⅓ of the highest contribution rate provided to a highly compensated employee

For example, assume a plan has only one highly compensated employee who earns the maximum compensation amount of $210,000 and receives an employer contribution allocation of $28,000. Since $28,000/$210,000 is 13.33%, the minimum gateway contribution for all eligible non-highly compensated employees in this plan is 4.44% (i.e. the one-third rule applies since it is the lesser amount). The following example will illustrate the power of a new comparability plan design.

Example 1: The RX Company has three categories of employees. First are two business owners who are 50% partners. Next are managers who are highly compensated employees due to their earnings. There are four managers. Finally there are support staff who provide clerical and administrative services to the company. There are 12 such support employees. The plan states that there are three groups of employees as outlined above, and that any employer contribution will be ratably allocated among the employees in the group. The plan also contains a 401(k) component and the company has always been able to pass the 401(k) non discrimination test. Listed below is an allocation of the 2005 contribution:

Name	Age	Compensation	Profit Sharing Contribution	401(k) Contribution	Total Allocation
Owner 1	49	$210,000	$28,000	$14,000	$42,000
Owner 2	48	$210,000	$28,000	$14,000	$42,000
Manager 1	50	$95,000	$0	$10,000	$10,000
Manager 2	48	$92,000	$0	$ 6,000	$ 6,000
Manager 3	45	$91,000	$0	$ 5,000	$ 5,000
Manager 4	42	$90,000	$0	$ 5,000	$ 5,000
Staff 1-6	35	$40,000	$1,778	$ 2,000	$ 3,778
Staff 7-12	30	$30,000	$1,334	$ 1,500	$ 2,834
Total		$1,208,000	$74,672	$75,000	$149,672

For purposes of the nondiscrimination test requirement, the equivalent benefit accrual rates (EBARs) are as follows:

Owner 1	5.11%
Owner 2	5.54%
Staff 1-6	5.34%
Staff 7-12	8.04%

All mangers (who are highly compensated employees) have a zero EBAR. The rate group tests are easily satisfied and the multi-tiered allocation formula is nondiscriminatory. What should be shown to the client or prospect is that absent this plan design and the desire to contribute the full $42,000 for the owners, there would have to be a profit sharing plan deposit of 13.33% of payroll or $161,067. Therefore, under this new comparability design the profit sharing plan contribution is reduced to $74,672 which is a difference of $86,395!

The Match Safe Harbor

The alternative to the 3% nonelective safe harbor contribution is the match safe harbor. Assuming the employer has met the notice requirements, simply *offering* the match safe harbor formula will qualify a plan to receive safe harbor treatment regardless of how many plan participants take advantage of it.

The required match formula is as based upon the following formula:

- For each $1 of elective deferral contribution made by the employee, the employer will match that deferral with $1, up to a maximum of 3% of compensation, plus

- For each additional $1 of elective deferral contribution over and above 3% of compensation, the employer will match 50 cents, to a maximum of 5% of compensation.

Example 1: Employee S makes $40,000 and elects to defer 2% of his compensation for a total of $800. The safe harbor contribution must be $800.

Example 2: Employee T makes $40,000 and elects to defer 4% of her compensation for a total of $1,600. The safe harbor matching contribution must be $1,400 (or 3.5% of compensation).

Example 3: Employee U makes $40,000 and does not contribute to the plan. The matching contribution for Employee U is $0.

Variations on this basic formula are permitted; for example, employers may use a straight 4% match (instead of matching 3% dollar for dollar and 2% at fifty cents on the dollar), so long as the ultimate result is at least the equivalent of the formula above.

The computation of the matching contribution can be made on either a monthly, quarterly, annual or "per pay period" basis.

Plans may make matching contributions in excess of the stated match formula (i.e., "enhanced matching contribution") above and continue to receive safe harbor treatment provided the following conditions apply:

- The matching contribution made on behalf of any employee may not be made with respect to any elective deferral contributions in excess of 6% of compensation.

- The rate of the matching contribution may not increase with the rate of the employee elective deferral contribution.

- The matching contribution with respect to any highly compensated employee at any rate of elective deferral is not greater than the matching contribution for any non-highly compensated employee.

Any matching contributions in excess of the limitations stated above will be subject to the nondiscrimination testing requirements.

Safe harbor plans may completely avoid the top-heavy minimum contribution requirement, provided there is no other employer contribution to the plan. Therefore, those plan sponsors who are looking to take advantage of the maximum 401(k) contribution, receive the safe harbor match (or an enhanced matching contribution) and not make any other employer contribution to the plan are good candidates for the match safe harbor plan.

SIMPLE 401(k) Plans

A second plan design that frees the employer from ADP/ACP testing, while maintaining the qualified plan structure of a 401(k) plan is the SIMPLE 401(k) plan (SIMPLE stands for "savings incentive match plan for employees.") SIMPLE 401(k) plans became available in 1997 but were largely overshadowed by the much more popular SIMPLE IRAs. The concept of safe harbor 401(k) design did not truly take hold until 1999, when safe harbor plans became available. SIMPLE 401(k) plans have the disadvantage of being subject to lower contribution and funding limits.

A SIMPLE 401(k) plan may be adopted only by an eligible employer, meaning an employer who has no more than 100 employees. Only employees earning $5,000 or more per year are counted, and once the level exceeds 100, the employer who has operated a SIMPLE 401(k) plan for at least a year will generally remain eligible for two additional years.

A SIMPLE 401(k) plan must also meet the the following requirements:

1.   The employer may not sponsor any other plan covering the same employees as those covered under the SIMPLE 401(k) plan,

2.   Elective deferrals and catch-up contributions are subject to lower limits, as described below;

3.   A matching or nonelective contribution must be made for every participant, and

3.   All contributions must be 100% vested at all times.

Contribution Requirements and Limits

Elective deferral contributions to a SIMPLE 401(k) plan are subject to the following limits:

Year	Elective Deferral Limit	Contribution Limit
2003	$ 8,000	$ 500
2004	$ 9,000	$1,500
2005	$10,000	$2,000
2006	indexed for inflation	$2,500

As with a safe harbor plan, the SIMPLE 401(k) contribution requirement can be met by either a nonelective contribution or a matching contribution. The nonelective employer contribution must be at least 2% of eligible compensation for all plan participants. Since this is *not* a matching contribution it is provided to all eligible employees regardless of their own level of participation. Eligible compensation for this purpose is limited as defined by Section 401(a)(17) of the Internal Revenue Code.

As an alternative to the 2% nonelective contribution, the employer may offer a matching formula. The match must be a dollar-for-dollar formula of up to 3% of compensation. Matching of catch-up contributions is not required.

SIMPLE 401(k) plans are much less flexible than safe harbor plans; no variation from these formulas is permitted. However, SIMPLE 401(k) contributions are not subject 25% of compensation deduction limit that applies to other 401(k) plans. SIMPLE 401(k) plans are also not subject to the top-heavy rules, provided they meet the foregoing requirements.

Chapter Endnotes

1.   Notice 2002-14, 2004-1 CB 548.

Chapter 6

The Devil is in the Details

A 401(k) plan is, without doubt, the best long-term tax deferred investment program available to Americans today. That is a carefully crafted sentence that we should pull apart to properly evaluate just what that means for those who have the opportunity to participate.

The 401(k) is widely recognized as the best tax deferred savings program available to those looking to save for retirement. Many other vehicles such as annuities, municipal bonds and life insurance provide tax deferred compounding, but these vehicles are typically funded with deposits that are made with after tax dollars. Thus, for the participant in a 33% tax bracket, a $3,000 deferral into a 401(k) plan must be compared to a $2,000 purchase of municipal bonds. In fact if an individual is saving money in any way other than through a 401(k) plan (or other tax-deferred vehicle), saving the same amount will result in greater take home pay currently. This point can be illustrated in the following example:

	Saver A	Saver B
Gross Income:	$40,000	$40,000
Savings in 401(k):	$ 3,000	$ 0
Savings outside Of 401(k):	$ 0	$ 3,000
Taxable Income:	$37,000	$40,000
Income Tax:	$11,111	$13,200
Net Spendable:	$25,889	$23,800
401(k) Advantage:	*$2,089*	

Having extolled the virtues of this wonderful savings program, let's review what saving in a 401(k) plan does *not* accomplish. A 401(k) plan is not a good place to save money to fund a vacation, plan for a wedding, or buy a new car. With several limited exceptions, it is generally not a good place to save for the purchase of a new home or the education of a child. As often stated in 401(k) enrollment meetings, this powerful savings vehicle is not akin to the old fashioned Christmas Club savings account.

When reading the opening sentence of this chapter, emphasis must be placed on the *long term* part of the statement. "Long term" should be defined as solely and primarily for retirement.

Nonetheless, there are several important instances where the account values can be accessed.

Distributions From 401(k) Plans

Although the primary purpose of a 401(k) plan is to accumulate money for retirement, there are plans that can, and in certain situations must, distribute money to a plan participant prior to actual retirement. This chapter will review the reasons for and consequences of such distributions.

Loans

A 401(k) plan may offer participants the ability to take loans from their accounts. Sole proprietors, S corp owners and partners were previously not allowed to take such loans but may do so under changes implemented in 2001.[1] Many plan sponsors offer a loan provision so that participants have the comfort of knowing they can access the funds if necessary. Figure 6.1 shows a sample loan agreement and document.

The law (Internal Revenue Code Section 72(p)) limits the amount that an individual can borrow from his or her account to the lesser of: one-half (½) the vested account balance *or* $50,000.

For purposes of applying the $50,000 loan limit, the greatest outstanding loan balance within the 12-month period prior to the loan request will be considered. For example, if an individual borrows $30,000 on January 1, 2004, makes regular loan repayments throughout 2004, the maximum amount available for a second loan on January 1, 2005 is $20,000.

FIGURE 6.1

PERSONAL AND CONFIDENTIAL

Mr. John Trustee
ABC Co.
123 Main Street
Anywhere, USA

RE:

Dear Mr. Trustee:

Enclosed please find an amortization schedule for. Please be sure to make him/her aware of the schedule of payments and copy us on all loan repayments. We strongly urge you to have the loan repayments through payroll deduction.

Please be advised that loan repayments are required to be made in accordance with the attached schedule. Failure to make loan repayments can result in a loan default and lead to taxes and penalties.

Please do not hesitate to call should you have any questions.

Sincerely,

Benefits Administrator

Enc.

FIGURE 6.1 (cont'd)

Section I - Loan Application for _____

Plan Name: _____

Participant MUST Complete A through C Below.

A. Loan Amount (Check one.)

    1. ❑ $_____ (Fill in a dollar amount)

        Note: Any amount exceeding the non-taxable loan limit will be considered taxable income.

    2. ❑ The maximum non-taxable amount available

B. Loan Terms (Complete 1, 2 and 3)

    1. Loan Term

        _____ years (Fill in a number)

        Note: The loan term can only exceed 5 years if the loan proceeds will be used to purchase a principal residence for the participant.

    2. Interest Rate

        _____% (Fill in a number)

    3. Repayment Schedule (Check one.)

        a. ❑ Fixed quarterly payments consisting of principal and interest
        b. ❑ Fixed monthly payments consisting of principal and interest
        c. ❑ Fixed weekly payments consisting of principal and interest

C. Participant Agreement

I agree to make interest and principal payments when due. I understand that failure to make such payments when due could jeopardize the status of this loan as a non-taxable transaction and could possibly result in the IRS treating these loan proceeds as a taxable distribution to me. I also understand that failure to repay this loan will reduce the benefits available to me from the retirement plan (by the amount of the outstanding loan balance plus accrued interest).

SIGNED x _____ **Date** _____
                                  Participant

Social Security Number:_____

FIGURE 6.1 (cont'd)

Section II - Loan Authorization

The Trustee is hereby authorized to make the loan as requested to the participant.

The loan proceeds should be obtained from the sale, liquidation or withdrawal of monies from the following asset(s): _____

_____

Note: Any readily available liquid cash asset(s) will be utilized first.

SIGNED x _____ **Date** _____
                          Authorized Company Representative

RETURN THIS FORM TO TRUSTEE

Spousal Consent

If Married, Spouse MUST Sign Consent and Have Signature Witnessed Below.

A. I am currently not married, and have not been married in the preceding 12 months.

SIGNED x _____ **Date** _____
                                          Participant

B. Spousal Consent

        I have been informed that this loan is secured by my spouse's vested accrued benefit under the plan. I realize that a failure to repay the loan may reduce the benefits available to my spouse and me upon my spouse's retirement or other termination of employment. Knowing this, I voluntarily consent to the loan of plan assets to my spouse according to the terms of this Loan Application.

        I agree to release and discharge the Trustee, Plan Administrator and Company from all liability for acting pursuant to this consent.

SIGNED x _____ **Date** _____
                                          Spouse

FIGURE 6.1 (cont'd)

C. Witness of Spousal Consent

Spousal consent must be witnessed by a Notary Public OR an Authorized Company Representative.
Witnessed by a Notary Public -OR- Witnessed by an Authorized Company Representative

Subscribed and sworn before me this ____day of _____, 20____

SIGNED X_____

Authorized Company Representative

Notary Public _____

State of _____ Date _____

My commission expires _____

RETURN THIS FORM TO TRUSTEE

Loans from 401(k) plans are required to be repaid over a 5-year period (or shorter if desired), unless the loan is for the purchase of a primary residence. The loan repayment period for a primary residence can mirror the amortization period of the primary mortgage. The loan interest rate can be "related to" the prime lending rate, usually one point above prime.

Since there are tax consequences for not repaying a loan in accordance with its terms, a well-established loan program will require that loan repayments be made through payroll deduction to avoid "loan defaults." Often this places additional administrative burden on the small plan sponsor who does not have a fully staffed human resources department.

If an individual were to consider a car loan, where interest would be paid to a financial institution, a loan from their 401(k) plan will allow repayments with a reasonable rate of interest to be paid back into the 401(k) account of the individual. At the same time, there is a certain amount of tax inefficiency with a 401(k) loan. More often than not, the interest paid under this approach is not deductible. The fact that all distributions taken from a plan are ultimately taxable means that the accumulated interest paid is effectively subject to double taxation. As with all financial transactions, the decision to use a plan loan should be compared against all available alternatives.

A loan default is deemed to occur if repayments are not made by the end of the calendar quarter after the quarter in which payments are due. For example if a payment that was due February 28 does not occur and is not made up prior to June 30 of that same year, the loan will be in default. The consequences of a loan default are the following:

- The outstanding balance of the loan is considered taxable income for the tax year in which the default occurs.

- If the participant is less than age 59½, a 10 percent penalty tax may apply in addition to the ordinary income tax.

- The loan outstanding at the time of default will continue to be outstanding in the event the participant wishes to take another loan from the plan at some point in the future. This can restrict the participant from taking another loan at some point in the future.

As of the writing of this chapter, a proposal to allow 401(k) participants to access their account balances via a "401(k) credit card" is under consideration.

Hardship Withdrawals

A 401(k) plan can also allow for withdrawals in the event of financial hardship. The plan administrator must exercise discretion in granting a withdrawal for this purpose, and be convinced that the plan participant would not have assess to the funds needed for the hardship from any other source (including a plan loan, if the plan so provides). A checklist for processing hardship withdrawals is shown at Figure 6.2.

Regulations list the following reasons as safe harbors to qualify for hardship:

- Purchase of a primary residence

- Higher education expenses

- Unreimbursed medical expenses

- Money needed to avoid eviction from a primary residence

FIGURE 6.2

Hardship Withdrawal Checklist

1.   Maximum Hardship Available Amount:

  a.   Elective Deferrals less.

  b.   Previous distributions of election deferrals plan.

  c.   Earnings credited to account through December 31, 1988.

2.   Immediate & heavy financial need:

  a.   Deemed immediate and heavy financial need:

  1.   Expenses for medical care that would be deductible under IRC Section. 213(d) (Without regard to 7.5% threshold).

  2.   Purchase of a principle residence.

  3.   Tuition, room, board up to next 12 months of post- secondary education for employee, employee's, spouse, children or dependents.*

  4.   Payments necessary to avoid eviction or foreclosure.

  5.   Burial/financial expenses for employee's deceased parent, spouse, children or dependents.*

  6.   Repair of damage to employee's principal residence that would qualify for casualty deduction under IRC Section 165 (without regard to 10% threshold).

  *Dependent as defined in section 152, without regard to 152 (b)(1), 152 (b)(2) & 152 (d)(1)(b).

3.   Questions for participant (to demonstrate need for plan withdrawal)

		Yes	No
a.	Do you have the ability to obtain funds through an insurance policy (or policies)?	_____	_____
b.	Can you liquidate personal assets?	_____	_____
c.	Can you satisfy your hardship withdrawals by ceasing of future elective deferrals?	_____	_____

FIGURE 6.2 (cont'd)

d.   Can you borrow from any qualified plan?   _____   _____

e.   Can you qualify for a commercial loan?   _____   _____

4.   I, (the participant) understand that I will not be able to make elective deferral contributions for at least 6 months after receipt of the hardship distribution.

_____

Participant Signature

- Funeral expenses

- Costs to repair casualty damage to a principal residence

Income taxes as well as excise taxes that would apply to distributions from a qualified plan apply to hardship withdrawals; however, the 20% required withholding tax that is typically applied to taxable distributions from qualified plans does not apply to hardship withdrawals.

A participant who takes a hardship withdrawal cannot make elective deferral contributions to the plan for at least six months.

Other events that can result in a distribution from the plan known as "distributable events" are:

- Death,

- Disability (as defined under the plan),

- Attainment of the plan's normal retirement age, and

- Termination of employment.

Tax Consequences of Distributions

In general, distributions paid from any qualified plan can be rolled over to another eligible retirement plan or individual retirement account (IRA). The most secure method of making a rollover is to have the monies transferred from the distributing plan to the eligible receiving plan (or IRA) directly. This type of rollover is called a direct rollover and is required to be offered in all qualified plans.

In the case of a direct rollover there is no withholding tax required. However if the payment is made to the individual participant (as opposed to the designated financial institution accepting the direct rollover) the requirement to withhold 20% must be enforced. If the individual participant does receive the payment and makes a rollover within 60 days, the entire distribution will be extended rollover treatment. However, since the 20% withholding would have already taken place, a reconciliation at year-end would be in order. A direct rollover is recommended in this case to avoid this complexity.

Any distribution that is not either rolled over by the plan trustee or the participant is subject to ordinary income tax for the calendar year in which the income is received. In addition, a 10% penalty tax may be imposed on distributions that are not rolled over if the distribution is paid prior to the age of 59½. There are exceptions to the 10% penalty tax provided in Section 72(t) as follows:

- Death,

- Disability,

- Separation from service and attainment of age 55,

- Substantially equal periodic payments (see below), and

- Qualified domestic relations order.

Substantially Equal Periodic Payments

IRS guidance[2] defines the conditions that will satisfy the "substantially equal periodic payment" exception under Section 72(t). First, once distributions commence under this exception, they must continue until the later of five years or attainment of age 59½. Should this pattern be broken, the 10% penalty tax would apply retroactively.

Substantially equal periodic payments will comply with the IRS requirements if the distributions are made in accordance with any of the three options listed below:

- Minimum distribution method: an annual payment is determined each year based on a single life or the joint lives of the participant and a beneficiary, under the rules for required minimum distributions;

- Fixed amortization method: a fixed annual payment is determined by amortizing the account balance in level amounts over a specified number of years, using the life expectancy and interest rates provided in the IRS guidance described above;

- Fixed annuitization method: a fixed annual payment is determined by dividing the individual's account balance by an annuity factor that is the present value of an annuity of $1 per year, beginning at the age of the individual in the first year of distribution.

The last option requires the use of a mortality table provide in IRS guidance, and in all cases involving interest the interest rates must fall within a corridor of current prevailing rates.

It is important to note that payments under the periodic payment exception can never be rolled over. Periodic payments under this exception are typically taken from IRAs. Under limited circumstances they may be available from a qualified plan, but in the case of a 401(k) plan, a series of periodic payments could be initiated only after a separation from service or other distributable events, not as an inservice distribution.

In Service Withdrawals

In general terms, funds in a 401(k) plan are accessible only under the four qualifying "distribitable events" of death, disability, termination or retirement. A unique feature of the profit sharing plan is a provision known as an in-service distribution. Under this provision, which must be provided for in the trust document, many plans allow participants to withdraw funds from their account and roll them into an IRA. Such a provision may be established for a separate profit sharing component, but not for 401(k) plan funds.

Plans Accepting Rollovers

Often plans allow for money to be rolled over into the plan from either another qualified plan or even an IRA. These funds should be accounted for in a separate account, not only because they are fully vested, but often they may be rolled out more easily than other funds in the account.

Minimum Distributions

Having reviewed the rules under which funds may be removed from a plan, we must now turn our attention to the times when you *must* take money out of a plan. The Internal Revenue Code plays a sensitive balancing act when it comes to retirement savings. Both IRAs and employer sponsored qualified plans (profit sharing, defined benefit, etc.) offer superior tax deferral, but all good things must truly come to an end.

There are some circumstances under which distributions have to be made. The most common of these applies to those participants who have attained the age of 70½. These individuals are generally required to take distributions as prescribed under the minimum distribution rules (Internal Revenue Code Section 401(a)(9)), as described below.

The minimum distribution rules effectively require that distributions be exhausted over the life expectancy (or the joint life expectancy of the participant and designated beneficiary). The required beginning date is the April 1 following the calendar year in which an individual attains age 70½ (see exception below).

FIGURE 6.3

Uniform Lifetime Table

Age of Employee	Distribution Period	Age of Employee	Distribution Period	Age of Employee	Distribution Period
70	27.4	86	14.1	101	5.9
71	26.5	87	13.4	102	5.5
72	25.6	88	12.7	103	5.2
73	24.7	89	12.0	104	4.9
74	23.8	90	11.4	105	4.5
75	22.9	91	10.8	106	4.2
76	22.0	92	10.2	107	3.9
77	21.2	93	9.6	108	3.7
78	20.3	94	9.1	109	3.4
79	19.5	95	8.6	110	3.1
80	18.7	96	8.1	111	2.9
81	17.9	97	7.6	112	2.6
82	17.1	98	7.1	113	2.4
83	16.3	99	6.7	114	2.1
84	15.5	100	6.3	115	1.9
85	14.8				

The amount of the distribution is determined by dividing the vested account balance as of the end of the previous year by the applicable life expectancy. The applicable life expectancy factor is generally taken from a Uniform Lifetime Table (see Figure 6.3) that appears in Treasury Regulation §1.401(a)(9)-9.

Final regulations issued in 2002 replaced earlier proposed regulations first issued in 1987 and revised in 2001. The final regulations were quite favorable compared to the earlier regulations in many ways—favorable in the sense that tax deferral of money held in a qualified plan account could last for a longer period of time than anyone would have expected. First, the life expectancy table provides for longer life expectancy factors than the tables previously in effect.

The Uniform Lifetime Table used for most lifetime distributions provides for life expectancy factors that are based upon the age of the participant and a beneficiary that is 10 years younger. The rules allow an even longer life expectancy for those participants whose spouse is the named beneficiary and is more than 10 years younger than the participant. Since a larger divisor means a smaller distribution, this means that these participants are permitted a longer payout period.

For those participants in a qualified plan who are not 5% owners, the required beginning date can be delayed until the April 1 following the calendar year in which the participant retires (unless the plan provides otherwise). Although the delay for non-5% owners applies to qualified plans and does not apply to individual retirement accounts (IRAs), EGTRRA 2001 also liberalized the rules for rollovers from IRAs to qualified plans. Therefore, someone who was required to withdraw money from an IRA due to attaining age 70½ and is still gainfully employed can make a rollover of the IRA balance into his or her employer's qualified plan (provided the plan is worded to accept such rollovers) and delay the additional taxable income that would otherwise have applied.

Minimum distributions have forced many planners to revisit the concept of always maximizing qualified plan deferrals in all circumstances. In particular, qualified plan assets are excellent sources of income for a participant and his or her spouse. Since plan assets are generally deposited on a pre-tax basis, and account balances are allowed to grow tax deferred, most accept the fact that withdrawals must have income taxes netted out. The traditional perspective is that the participant may certainly be in a lower tax bracket when making these withdrawals – but there is also the ability to control the flow of funds as they are taken out.

For non-spouse beneficiaries, these funds may often create a significant, and often unexpected, tax burden, particularly since nonspouses have no ability to roll over the funds. The rude awakening comes in the form of two accumulated taxes. In addition to ordinary income tax, many account balances will also be subject to an estate tax. Under current law, this tax can be as much as 47% (in 2005). Applying the associated maximum federal income tax bracket (35% in 2005), state income taxes (assuming 7%, but higher in some states), and probate fees (3% in some cases), many larger accounts have been diminished by as over 75% when passed on to children or other heirs, (even with offsetting of some of the taxes as income in respect of a decedent).

Very often, the money that has accumulated in a qualified plan (or IRA) is a substantial asset after retirement in terms of an individual's taxable estate. Money that remains in a qualified plan or IRA at the time of a participant's death can pose certain tax problems if not properly planned for. An untimely death can cause the money that has accumulated for years without any income or estate taxes to become subject to these taxes in a single taxable year. Many practitioners consider the assets that have accumulated on a tax- deferred basis to be "illiquid" at the time of death, due to the potential heavy tax burden that could come all at once. If money has to be withdrawn from an IRA or qualified plan account to pay estate taxes, that money is also subject to income taxes which can be as much as a 75% shrinkage factor under the tax law today.

With proper planning this result can be avoided. In fact, under the right circumstances, the wealth of an individual and his or her heirs can be a multiple of the original account balance (measured from the required beginning date). It is important to consider this opportunity when communicating to individuals with substantial account balances. The example below highlights a common situation where the lack of planning or the right planning can make a difference worth millions of dollars.

> *Example:* John Smith has an IRA account with a balance of $1 million and is 75 years old. He has named his wife Jane aged 72 as the primary beneficiary of the IRA in the event of his death. John has been taking minimum distributions since age 70½.

> Assume John dies and Jane continues to take distributions from John's IRA for the rest of her life. Jane's distributions will now be based over her single life expectancy (15.5 years at age 72—see Figure 6.4). Assume that the total of the minimum distributions paid to Jane from the point of John's

death is $1,438,571 based upon a 5% rate of return, and that Jane lives to her life expectancy. Alternatively, Jane is given guidance that upon John's death, she is permitted to make a rollover of the entire balance to her own spousal IRA. With this rollover comes the ability for Jane to designate her own beneficiaries, and that she names her 5-year old granddaughter. At the end of the 15-year period (Jane's life expectancy) instead of the IRA being depleted, there remains a balance of $831,571. This $831,571 balance can now be paid over the remaining life expectancy of the granddaughter, which at age 20 is approximately 66 years. The distributions that would have been paid out since John's death will now be increased from $1,438,571 to $6,918,971 for an increase of $5,480,400!

This planning strategy is sometimes referred to as a "stretch IRA." In order for this strategy to come to life there needs to be additional planning as referred to above. The money in John and Jane's IRA accounts needs to remain in place for the life expectancies of the beneficiaries. This will prolong the income tax deferral that can last for generations.

Chapter Endnotes

1. See IRC Sec 4975(f)(6). This change took effect beginning after 2001.
2. Rev. Rul. 2002-62, 2002-2 CB 710.

Single Life Table

Age	Life Expectancy	Age	Life Expectancy	Age	Life Expectancy
0	82.4	38	45.6	75	13.4
1	81.6	39	44.6	76	12.7
2	80.6	40	43.6	77	12.1
3	79.7	41	42.7	78	11.4
4	78.7	42	41.7	79	10.8
5	77.7	43	40.7	80	10.2
6	76.7	44	39.8	81	9.7
7	75.8	45	38.8	82	9.1
8	74.8	46	37.9	83	8.6
9	73.8	47	37.0	84	8.1
10	72.8	48	36.0	85	7.6
11	71.8	49	35.1	86	7.1
12	70.8	50	34.2	87	6.7
13	69.9	51	33.3	88	6.3
14	68.9	52	32.3	89	5.9
15	67.9	53	31.4	90	5.5
16	66.9	54	30.5	91	5.2
17	66.0	55	29.6	92	4.9
18	65.0	56	28.7	93	4.6
19	64.0	57	27.9	94	4.3
20	63.0	58	27.0	95	4.1
21	62.1	59	26.1	96	3.8
22	61.1	60	25.2	97	3.6
23	60.1	61	24.4	98	3.4
24	59.1	62	23.5	99	3.1
25	58.2	63	22.7	100	2.9
26	57.2	64	21.8	101	2.7
27	56.2	65	21.0	102	2.5
28	55.3	66	20.2	103	2.3
29	54.3	67	19.4	104	2.1
30	53.3	68	18.6	105	1.9
31	52.4	69	17.8	106	1.7
32	51.4	70	17.0	107	1.5
33	50.4	71	16.3	108	1.4
34	49.4	72	15.5	109	1.2
35	48.5	73	14.8	110	1.1
36	47.5	74	14.1	111	1.0
37	46.5				

Chapter 7

Asset Allocation 101

No book on 401(k) plans would be complete without at least one chapter on investments. The growth in popularity of 401(k) plans – and their self-directed style of investing — has been one of the most significant single factors influencing the capital markets. According to the Investment Company Institute (ICI), 45% of all investments in mutual funds are represented by accounts that are classified as retirement accounts.[1]

Totaling over $12 trillion in wealth as of December 2003, almost half of these investments are in self-directed, investor controlled accounts. One would assume that these investors represent a fairly savvy crowd.

From our experience, one can never assume that the plan participant has a sufficient working knowledge of investments to properly manage their own assets. The key to any good 401(k) enrollment meeting is a solid review of the basics of investing.

Once the employee deferrals and possibly some additional company deposits are safely tucked away in a tax deferred vehicle – what happens next? Many financial planners have always considered the miracle of compound interest as the cornerstone of making money grow. This magic can even be more potent when applied within the context of a tax-deferred vehicle.

For a simplified and easy to remember method of calculating how fast money doubles, refer to the Rule of 72. Under this mathematical formula, to determine how many years it will take for money to double at a specific rate of interest, simply divide the number 72 by the presumed return. The result is how many years it will take the opening balance to double. For example, at a rate of 6%, money will double every 12 years. Similarly, at the rate of 8%, money will double in nine years. Of course, one must recall that when projecting a 401(k) balance, typically future deposits are made into the account. Although the simplicity of the Rule of 72 does not readily accommodate future deposits, it can be a quick method to determine how rapidly your existing account may double.

The key to having your account grow can be proper asset allocation.[2]

Based upon several key types of asset classes, asset allocation worships at the altar of diversification. Under this approach, investment alternatives are broken into two main categories: bonds and equities. The best distinction between bonds and stocks comes from Nick Murray, who asks all of his clients – "Do you prefer to be a loaner or an owner?"[3]

Quite simply, equities involve owning a piece of a company, and bonds involve loaning funds out (to companies, institutions, or governments). There is a place for both, and there is true value in understanding enough about each to make some wise investment decisions.

Bonds

Bonds are often called income or debt instruments. Bonds involve lending an institution or corporation money. The basic return that a bond or bond fund will deliver to one's account is the result of interest being paid on the money loaned to the institution. The loan is created for a specified number of years at a stated rate of interest. At the end of the duration, the initial amount "loaned" is repaid to the individual.

If bonds are held to maturity, the only risk that they represent to a portfolio is credit risk (the probability that at the end of the bond duration, the receiving institution will repay the initial debt). For this reason, bonds are often seen as a less risky or more conservative class of investment than equities.

This distinction can often be an oversimplification, though, as some forms of debt can actually be riskier than investing in the stock of a large, stable company. Bonds are often mistakenly categorized as no-risk investments. Even a government bond, which is backed by the full faith and credit of the federal government (and its ability to raise revenue via taxation) can present investment risk, or may even go down in value.

The second element of risk is interest rate risk, which is borne out of the fact that rates change frequently (actually daily within the bond market). Quite simply, since rates change, the appeal of a particular bond (or note) changes on a daily basis. Assume you buy a ten-year bond that is issued at a rate of 8%. Several years later, the market rate for a similar bond has changed, actually dropping to 6%. Would a new investor looking to buy a bond rather own a new bond at 6%, or perhaps be willing to buy your bond, which pays 8%? Would he or she be willing to pay you a premium, resulting in an increase in your return?

Let's assume that you opted not to sell your bond, realizing that if you did, you would no longer have an investment that paid you 8%. Two more years down the road, rates are back up. In fact, they have risen to 10%. You decide to call your buddy who almost bought your bond a few years back and see if there is still any interest (no pun intended) in working out a deal. At this stage, the premium is gone because a new bond will pay more than yours does. The net effect is that your bond is trading at a discount. You owe him more money to buy your bond. Should you be forced to sell, you will actually experience a loss, getting less back than the initial amount invested into the bond.

Welcome to the world of the bond markets …and welcome to the reason that bonds *not* held to maturity may present more investment risk than is typically understood. As an aside – bond *funds* are much more prone to this risk. Why? Because the control of the buying and selling of individual issues is no longer in the hands of the individual, but rather in the hands of a bond manager, whose bonus is based more upon annual return than upon the same 30 year history that is meaningful to many 401(k) investors.

Types of Bonds

Recalling that bonds are essentially forms of debt, there are several variations or flavors to consider. The most significant variation is to whom the funds are being loaned. As with most markets, the greater the potential risk, the greater the return (in this case, interest rate). Often also referred to as capital preservation instruments, bonds vary in class almost as much as equities. Ranked in order of relative risk, bond types are as follows:

Government Bonds. As the name implies, these involve lending funds to the United States government. These bonds have the lowest amount of credit risk among all asset classes. This is due to the fact that the best-proven money raising machine known to mankind is the United States government. Backed by the full faith and credit of the United States, there is virtually no chance that a government bond will either miss an interest payment or fail to be repaid. Foreign governments also issue debt, which is typically in their local currency and based upon their ability to tax in order to make payments. More on currency risk later.

Municipal bonds are similar to government bonds except that state and local governments issue them. As such, their creditworthiness is slightly less than federal debt, but make no mistake about it, these guys can tax themselves out of a hole, too. Typically the interest received on these notes is income tax free. In exchange for this advantage, the rate is typically set lower than a taxable instrument. Due to this lower rate, and the fact that qualified plans do not pay tax on their income, these bonds are rarely used in 401(k) plans or other retirement programs.

Corporate bonds involve lending funds to corporate entities. These funds are used for growth and reinvestment back into the organizations or to fund special projects. The company sets the rate, but the market is fairly efficient in evaluating whether or not a rate is competitive, given the health of the issuing company and other prevailing rates at a given point in time. As far as asset classes are concerned, there are domestic bonds, international bonds and global bonds. Domestic bonds are issued from firms headquartered in the United States, international bonds are issued by firms headquartered anywhere in the world besides the United States, and global bonds represent a hybrid of corporate debt issued anywhere in the world.

In the event that the company is forced to liquidate, bondholders are the first creditors to receive payment. Some bonds are convertible, which means that either at the bondholder's discretion, or when the decision is forced by the issuer, the bonds may be converted into equity within that corporation. Bonds are rated by several various rating agencies. Ratings provide the investor with an assessment of the credit worthiness of a firm. Gradations vary by rating agency, but it is a good idea to familiarize yourself with the rating system and use this as a method of determining part of the risk associated with a particular bond.

High yield (junk) bonds came into popularity during the 1980s when higher risk and growing companies began to issue debt. Given the greater risk of default, these firms offered above market rates of interest. These are clearly at the highest end of the risk curve for bonds. From a risk perspective, many believe that this asset class is more like the risk associated with an equity fund.

Equities

There is an old adage in the investment world: "Do you prefer being a loaner or an owner?" Investing in stocks involves equity ownership in a company. As such, stockholders are entitled to elect the board of directors and vote on significant matters affecting the company's operations. Ownership also reflects sharing in the operating profits of the company; either in the form of dividends or appreciation in the value of the company itself (expressed in the stock price).

Historically, equities have outperformed bonds as an asset class. From 1928 to year-end 2004, the average annual return of the most stable stock index (the Dow Jones Industrial Average) was 10.2%.[4] Nonetheless, many have also learned (often the hard way) that "past performance is not an indication of future performance." Translated, this means you could lose it all. Equities represent the opportunity to gain *and* to lose. Knowing the various asset classes is the first step towards investing wisely.

Equity classes are split into two main areas: growth and value. Growth represents companies that are healthy, operating in a growth mode, and tend to have stable profits – a factor also reflected in the market. Most of the future increase in the stock price is expected to come from the growth in company profits and market share.

Conversely, a value stock is one that may be currently undervalued by the marketplace. These firms tend to have lower P/E (price to earnings) ratios. Translated, earnings of the firm may be somewhat lower. The company may be in an expansion or development mode. Book values of the firms tend to be lower and overall these firms are less mature than growth companies.

Following the delineation based upon value or growth, companies are further classified based upon size. Each classification is determined by the company's capitalization ("cap") size. No, this is not a category to determine the head size of the CEO. "Cap" size means multiplying the share price by the number of shares outstanding to arrive at the capitalization value of a company. In a very real sense, it represents the value of a company.

Just like baseball caps, corporate stocks are classified as small, medium or large caps. Large cap firms are deemed to have a market value of more than $10 billion. Medium capitalization is defined as ranging from $2 billion to $10 billion and small cap is designated as under $2 billion. (Of late, a fourth category known as "micro cap" has become prevalent as well). We will keep our focus on the big three.

International equities represent ownership in firms that are domiciled outside of the United States. Just like U.S.-based firms, they can be classified by growth versus value and by cap size. These investments are often classified as riskier investments given the currency risk. Specifically, you are buying shares in U.S. dollars, and converting them into the currency of the country where the firm is domiciled. Your investment must always be converted back into dollars to determine the proper value.

For example, an Italian stock may appreciate by 4%, but actually lose the U.S. investor money if the dollar drops in value against the Euro. The presence of these two moving pieces forces many to immediately classify any international investment as the most aggressive of all asset classes.

The Mighty Mutual Fund

For the time being, the overwhelming majority of 401(k) investment choices are provided through mutual funds. Thus, the average 401(k) investor is assessing equity and bond funds rather than individual issues. A mutual fund is simply a basket of stocks or bonds owned in a common form (i.e., by a company) and bundled into one neat package. Divided into shares, each share represents an equal interest in the underlying investments. The price of a single share is determined daily as the underlying stocks or bonds change in value.

When investing in a mutual fund, a significant factor to consider is what type of fund it is and how the underlying investments are classified. One of the best tools for classifying mutual funds has been developed by Morningstar.

For this purpose, we will utilize the Morningstar system of asset classification. The basic variations have already been shared (growth and value stocks) and further refined in to the categories of large cap, medium cap and small cap. Adding the style category or blend creates the horizontal categories of Morningstar's trademarked nine-grid "style box." Along the vertical, the capitalization of a firm is indicated. From top to bottom, the capitalization categories are large, medium and small.

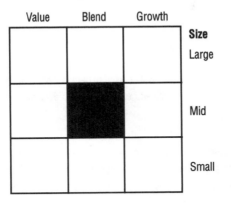

Morningstar Style Box™*

The Forgotten Asset Class

Many investment allocation models ignore the category of real estate. In many ways, real estate embodies aspects of both categories (i.e., equities and bonds) because there is a steady stream of rental income (like a bond coupon) and a speculative piece of upside (or downside) potential (like a share of stock). The most convenient way for the average investor to participate in real estate as an investment is through a real estate investment trust (REIT).

Many feel that REITs are a particularly good asset to be included in one's IRA or retirement plan.[5] In particular, equity REITs provide the potential for market appreciation as well as the steady rental income traditionally favored by real estate investors.

Many devotees of asset allocation feel that REITs can actually enhance portfolio return while decreasing risk when properly positioned within an asset allocated portfolio. For purposes of our discussion, we will not ignore REITs, but place them instead into the equity income category.

FIGURE 7.2

SAMPLE RISK PROFILE QUESTIONNAIRE

Client Name: _____

Amount: _____

Your answers to the following questions will be used to generate the asset allocation model most appropriate to help you achieve your stated goals, taking into account your investment horizon and tolerance for risk.

1. Your investment objective summarizes the primary purpose of your account. It serves to define how assets should be managed. When asking yourself, "What do I want most to accomplish?", select the objective that best fits the purpose of your account.

    ❏ Preserve asset value
    ❏ Generate high current income
    ❏ Achieve asset growth with moderate current income
    ❏ Achieve strong asset growth with nominal income
    ❏ Achieve maximum capital appreciation

2. Check the box that indicates your response to the following statement: I am comfortable with investments that may go down in value from time to time, if they offer the potential for higher returns.

    ❏ Strongly disagree
    ❏ Disagree
    ❏ Somewhat agree
    ❏ Agree
    ❏ Strongly agree

3. Age is a critical determinant of portfolio selection. Please check your age in the box below.

    ❏ 35 and under
    ❏ 36 – 45
    ❏ 46 – 55
    ❏ 56 – 64
    ❏ 65 and over

FIGURE 7.2 (cont'd)

4. Your investment time horizon is an important variable to consider when constructing your portfolio. How long will it be before you start taking withdrawals?

    ❏   0 – 1 year
    ❏   1 – 2 years
    ❏   2 – 4 years
    ❏   4 – 6 years
    ❏   More than 6 years

5. Once you begin taking withdrawals, how long will the money in the account have to last before it is depleted?

    ❏   It will be a lump sum withdrawal
    ❏   Less than 1 year
    ❏   1 – 5 years
    ❏   6 – 10 years
    ❏   11 years or more

6. Assessing your income requirements is essential in determining the appropriate asset allocation for your account. Please check the box that best approximates the amount of CURRENT income your account will need to generate annually as a percentage of your total income from all sources.

    ❏   0 – 5%
    ❏   6 – 15%
    ❏   16 – 30%
    ❏   31 – 50%
    ❏   Over 50%

7. How long could you cover monthly living expenses, (i.e. mortgage, car, food & utility bills) with cash and liquid investments you currently have on hand?

    ❏   1 month or less
    ❏   1 – 3 months
    ❏   3 – 6 months
    ❏   6 – 12 months
    ❏   More than 12 months

FIGURE 7.2 (cont'd)

8.   What is your prediction for your future income from sources other than investments over the next ten years?

     ❏   It will decrease greatly
     ❏   It will decrease slowly
     ❏   It will stay the same
     ❏   It will increase slowly
     ❏   It will increase greatly

9.   What type of account are you opening?

     ❏   IRA (Individual Retirement Account)
     ❏   Pension account
     ❏   Regular after-tax account
     ❏   Section 529 account
     ❏   Combination of these accounts

10.   What is your Federal Tax Bracket?

     ❏   15%
     ❏   25%
     ❏   28%
     ❏   33%
     ❏   35%

11.   State of Residence _____.

Client Signature _____ Date: _____

Representative Signature _____ Date: _____

Asset Allocation and Risk

Of course, as any beginning investor knows, the amount of potential risk an investment has is directly related to the amount of potential return that is available within that investment. Unlocking that return within the best confines of each investor's comfort level is squarely based upon the concept of asset allocation. Asset allocation is quite simply the diversification of an investment account among several of the different asset classes we have just reviewed.

The core of asset allocation is risk tolerance. In order to manage risk, one must determine how much of it should be taken. The financial markets operate along two parallel seesaws. On the quantifiable statistical side there is the balance of risk and return. On the human behavior side are the competing emotions of fear and greed. Gauging the interplay of each, as well as how they change during the course of a plan participant's career, is the central role of gauging risk tolerance.

The responses to the questions in Figure 7.2 are placed into a scoring system, with the results tallied into one of six categories. There are 10 scored answers on the above questionnaire. One to five points are ascribed to each of the listed options within each question (one point for the first option, two for the second, etc). Using the following grid, a basic risk tolerance is established according to the following range:

0 – 9 points	-	Conservative Income Investor
10-19 points	-	Income Investor
20-29 points	-	Conservative Growth Investor
30-39 points	-	Growth Investor
40-49 points	-	Aggressive Growth Investor

A little later in this chapter we will review the particulars of each classification and how the asset classes are allocated into each category.

Measuring Investment Risk

Risk is a relative term. When determining risk, one always must ask "compared to what." There are several key terms that investment professionals use to gauge and determine risk. We will look at three of these, *beta, standard deviation,* and the *Sharpe ratio.*

Beta is a term that compares the risk of a fund to the appropriate market index. For a large cap stock fund, the appropriate index is the S&P 500. Assuming that the index is rated a risk of 1.0, then the fund in question is deemed to have a beta greater or less than 1.0. A fund with a beta of less than 1.0 is deemed to be less volatile than the S&P 500. Specifically, a fund with a beta of .80 is deemed to be 20% less risky than the S&P 500 index. Conversely, a beta in excess of the index results in the determination that a fund is riskier than the S&P 500 index.

Standard deviation is another tool for comparing a fund to the relative index. Typically calculated over a period of time, standard deviation is a rather complex formula that provides a measure of volatility as compared to the index. Thus if a fund has a standard deviation in excess of an index, the fund can be deemed to be more volatile than that index. Investments themselves have standard deviation in relation to each other. Typically they reflect a range of returns experienced by an investment for a given period of time. A government bond has a relatively low standard deviation, whereas a junk bond fund will have a higher standard deviation.

The Sharpe Ratio is the third and final tool for our essential investment toolkit. The concept was developed by Professor William Sharpe as his contribution to the development of "Modern Portfolio Theory" that guides most investment professionals today. Without getting into the mathematics of the steps, you simply need to know that the ratio is a direct measure of reward to risk. Essentially, the ratio will provide an assessment of how much additional potential return is available in exchange for trailing a certain amount of risk. The higher a Sharpe ratio, the greater the possibility of a positive return.

At the risk of oversimplification, the ideal fund would be one with a low beta, low standard deviation and a high Sharpe ratio. Easier said than done, the trick is to first find such a fund, know when to buy it, then know when to sell it.

Cutting the Pie

Once the ability to tolerate risk has been assessed and quantified, the next step is to determine the best asset allocation associated with a determined risk profile, spread among the basic asset classes. Figure 7.3 shows five sample allocations that correlate to the categories established under the risk questionnaire.

A final word about investment risk and asset allocation. Many people misgauge their investment strategy based upon their perceived time horizon. They adopt an asset allocation mix designed solely to get them to age 65. Proper asset allocation will carry an individual through their working years and well into retirement. Using age 65 as normal retirement age, the average person still has a life expectancy of at least 20 years. Thus, 20 – 30 years needs to become the anticipated investment horizon.

Chapter Endnotes

1. *Fundamentals: Investment Company Institute Research in Brief,* p. 2 (Investment Company Institute, Vol. 13, No. 2, June 2004), at: www.ici.org.
2. Burton Malkiel, *A Random Walk Down Wall Street* (W.W. Norton & Company, Inc. January 2004).
3. Nick Murray, *The Nick Murray Reader* (Nick Murray, Mattituck, NY), at: www.nickmurray.securities.com.
4. George Thurnburg, Thornburg Investment Management, *Commentary* (December 2004).
5. Neuberger Berman and Heidi L. Steiger, *Wealthy and Wise* (John Wiley & Sons, October 2002). See Chapter 12, Richard Adler, *Adding Real Estate to Your Investment Mix.*

FIGURE 7.3

ALLOCATION OF ASSETS IN CONSERVATIVE INCOME

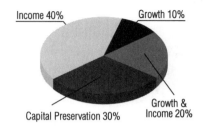

Income 40%   Growth 10%

Growth &
Income 20%

Capital Preservation 30%

Historical returns for a conservative income portfolio of this allocation would be as follows:

3 Mos	1 Year	3 Years	5 Years	10 Years[1]
2.21	4.70	5.22	6.13	8.11

ALLOCATION OF ASSETS IN AN INCOME PORTFOLIO

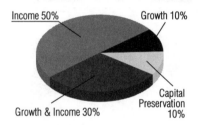

Income 50%   Growth 10%

Capital
Preservation
10%

Growth & Income 30%

Historical returns for an income portfolio with this allocation would be as follows:

3 Mos	1 Year	3 Years	5 Years	10 Years[2]
2.79	5.88	6.57	7.60	9.75

ALLOCATION OF ASSETS IN A CONSERVATIVE PORTFOLIO

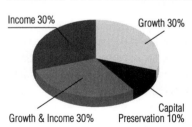

Income 30%   Growth 30%

Capital
Preservation 10%

Growth & Income 30%

Historical returns for a conservative growth portfolio of this allocation are:

3 Mos	1 Year	3 Years	5 Years	10 Years[3]
4.96	8.25	7.39	7.69	11.81

FIGURE 7.3 (cont'd)

ALLOCATION OF ASSETS IN A GROWTH PORTFOLIO

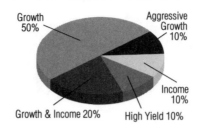

Growth 50%
Aggressive Growth 10%
Income 10%
Growth & Income 20%
High Yield 10%

Historical returns for a growth portfolio of this allocation would be as follows:

3 Mos	1 Year	3 Years	5 Years	10 Years[4]
7.03	10.37	7.47	7.75	13.49

ALLOCATION OF ASSETS IN AN AGGRESSIVE GROWTH PORTFOLIO

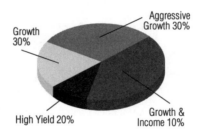

Aggressive Growth 30%
Growth 30%
High Yield 20%
Growth & Income 10%

Historical returns for an aggressive growth portfolio of this allocation are:

3 Mos	1 Year	3 Years	5 Years	10 Years[5]
9.93	14.88	11.24	8.59	14.76

1. Based upon indicated allocation at December 31, 2004. *Source –Morningstar Principia*
2. Based upon indicated allocation at December 31, 2004. *Source –Morningstar Principia*
3. Based upon indicated allocation at December 31, 2004. *Source –Morningstar Principia*
4. Based upon indicated allocation at December 31, 2004. *Source –Morningstar Principia*
5. Based upon indicated allocation at December 31, 2004. *Source –Morningstar Principia*

Chapter 8

Plan Features

No single aspect of the retirement planning process is as misunderstood as the area of plan features and the various product options. This is particularly true in the world of 401(k) plans. All in all, over $12 trillion of the market's $22 trillion in total value is contained in qualified plans.[1] Before we review the overall marketplace, and the changes we anticipate seeing over the next few years, a review of the existing regulations and guidelines is in order.

Once employees have been provided with the opportunity to directly manage their own accounts, the next critical item becomes providing them access to those accounts. Most modern plans afford participants with a variety of methods to determine central elements of their account. Via either an internet access site, voice response unit or a central customer service line, employees can determine details such as such as account balance (typically as of the last market close), current asset allocation, loan information, and recent transaction information. Most necessary account maintenance functions can be handled such as beneficiary changes, deferral changes, projection of retirement needs, asset allocation planning, and so on.

ERISA Section 404(c)

Section 404(c) of the Employee Retirement Income Security Act of 1974 (ERISA) sets forth the types of information that must be provided to participants, as well as additional information that must be made available upon request. If the plan complies with these requirements, plan fiduciaries will generally be shielded from liability under the fiduciary responsibility provisions of ERISA for any loss that results from the participant's exercise of control.

Required Information for Plan Participants

The following information must be provided by the plan fiduciary to each plan participant (or beneficiary, if applicable):

1. An explanation that the plan intends to constitute an ERISA Section 404(c) plan, as described in the regulation, and that the fiduciaries of the plan may be relieved of liability for any losses that are the direct and necessary result of investment instructions given by the participant.

2. A description of the investment options available under the plan and, with respect to each designated investment alternative, a general description of the investment objectives and risk and return characteristics of each opinion, including information relating to the type and diversification of assets comprising the portfolio of the designated investment options.

3. If relevant, identification of any designated investment managers.

4. An explanation of the circumstances under which participants may give investment instructions under the terms of the plan, including any restrictions on transfers to or from a designated investment option, and any restrictions on the exercise of voting, tender and similar rights that may apply to a participant's investment in the investment option.

5. With respect to each investment option available under the plan, a description of any transaction fees and expenses that affect the participant's account balance in connection with the purchase or sale of interests in that investment (e.g., commissions, sales loads, deferred sales charges, redemption or exchange fees).

6. Identification of the plan fiduciary (and, if applicable, any person or persons designated by the plan fiduciary) responsible for providing the information described in the 404(c) regulation upon the request of a participant and a description of the information described in the regulation, which may also be obtained on request.

7. In the case of plans that offer employer stock or other employer securities as an investment alternative, a description of the procedures

established to provide for the confidentiality of information relating to such investments by participants and the identification of the plan fiduciary responsible for monitoring compliance with those procedures.

8.   For any investment option that is subject to the Securities Act of 1933, immediately following a participant's initial investment, the plan must provide a copy of the most recent prospectus.

9.   Subsequent to a participant's investment in an option under the plan, any materials provided to the plan relating to the exercise of voting, tender or similar rights that are incidental to the participant holding of an ownership interest in that investment alternative in his or her individual account, to the extent that those rights are passed through to participants under the terms of the plan.

Additional Information for Plan Participants

In addition to the preceding, which is required, the following information should be available to the participant and beneficiary upon request:

- A description of the annual operating expenses of each designated investment alternative.

- Copies of any prospectuses, financial statements and reports, and any other materials relating to investment alternatives available under the plan, to the extent that the information is provided to the plan.

- A list of the assets comprising the portfolio of the designated investment alternative that constitutes plan assets, the value of each asset (or the proportion of the investment alternative that it comprises), and, with respect to each such asset that is a fixed-rate investment contract issued by a bank (e.g., savings and loan association) or insurance company, the name of the issuer of the contract, the term of the contract and the rate of return on the contract.

Investment Policy Statements

Having reviewed the basics of asset allocation and how an employee may choose to diversify their portfolio (see Chapter 7), a few words should be said about how the actual menu of investment choices is developed. By one recent count, there were over 26,000 mutual funds available on the various exchanges in the United States (including various share classes for some funds).[2] ERISA Section 404(c) requires that a minimum of four investment options, plus a liquid (money market) account be offered. Most plan sponsors consider between 10 and 30, at most, to be a reasonable number of choices. So how does one narrow 26,000 down to between 10 and 30 options?

Enter the Investment Policy Statement. This document reflects the stated objectives of the investment committee or governing body of the plan (trustees) as it relates to what investment classes and categories they deem suitable as offerings made within the program. For the nonself-directed plan, this document is a crucial (and often overlooked) piece. For the 401(k) plan it is a wonderful tool to be utilized when performing the required due diligence set forth in Section 404(c).

A sample Investment Policy Statement is shown in Figure 8.1. Some are more complex, detailing expense ratios, performance metrics, greater detail of asset classifications, etc., while others are even simpler. The best choice, particularly for a self-directed 401(k) plan, is one that raises the issues and questions the trustees must properly consider. It should provide them with the latitude to make an informed decision, but set the standards by which the group should perform their analysis and make their ultimate decision.

Fidelity Bonds

What other ways do trustees have, or are required, to transfer plan liability? The fidelity bond, or surety bond—often misunderstood, and even more often disregarded—is a requirement for all qualified plans that cover anyone other than a single employee.

Provided by property and casualty carriers, often in conjunction with an overall business liability policy, the fidelity bond protects plan participants from malfeasance or fraud committed by the trustees or anyone else handling money for the plan. Examples include taking off with the funds, misappropriation of funds, improper payment of plan balances to terminees and some procedural violations. A fidelity bond *does not* protect participants from poor investment selections or the loss of assets due to poor investment decisions.

FIGURE 8.1

Sample Investment Policy Statement

Plan and Trust Name: _____ ("Plan"). This Investment Policy Statement is adopted for the Plan by _____ (Plan Fiduciary). The Plan provides for individual accounts and permits participants (or beneficiaries) to exercise investment control over the assets in their accounts.

The Plan's overall investment objective is to provide Plan participants (or beneficiaries) with a sufficient variety of investment options to enable participants to achieve their individual investment goals for retirement. To accomplish this, the Plan may enter into group annuity contracts or agreements with financial services providers that offer a wide variety of investment options and benefit distribution facilities. The investment options should represent multiple asset classes covering equity (stock), fixed income (bond), money market, stable value, and balanced options. These investments will have the following general characteristics:

- Different risk/return characteristics

- Different investment objectives and styles

- Annualized returns over three-, five- and ten-year periods that have met or exceeded the competitive averages or established industry benchmarks

- Reasonable total expenses that are disclosed to participants

The selection of particular investment options will be based on specific criteria or standards described in an attachment to this document which will form a part of the Investment Policy Statement. It is the intent to have investment options that represent a diversified mix of asset classes and styles, comprising approximately _____ choices. Included in the selections: active and passive/index-like options, equity options across capitalization ranges (small, mid and large capitalization) and style categories (growth, blend and value) as well as international equity exposure (foreign or global). Income options will focus on credit quality (investment grade, high yield) and maturity period (short, intermediate, long term).

The Plan's service provider should provide detailed account statements that regularly inform participants regarding investment performance and expenses that affect their individual account balances. The Plan intends to comply with ERISA Section 404(c) regulations. The choice of investment options and services provided to the Plan should facilitate compliance. In addition, to the extent provided in the Plan, participants may exercise any voting, tender or other rights connected with investments in their accounts.

FIGURE 8.1 (cont'd)

This Investment Policy Statement will be reviewed _____ times a year to monitor the performance and characteristics of each investment option available under the Plan and to determine
the continued appropriateness of the investment options available to participants. Factors that
will be considered in this review include actual returns net of expenses, risk-adjusted performance, and any changes to risk and style characteristics or level of fees. Any investment fund
that fails to meet its investment criteria for a period of _____ may be removed
as an option from the Plan and a substitute fund with similar characteristics may be added.

This Investment Policy Statement is adopted on behalf of the Plan as of (date).

_____   _____

Plan Fiduciary(ies) Signature(s)   Date

A plan must maintain a bond equal to at least 10% of plan assets. These bonds
are relatively inexpensive and are often placed in 3-year increments. There is usually a minimum bond size of $10,000 – so smaller plans often exceed the 10%
minimum limit and simply "grow into" the 10% minimum coverage. Those handling or having access to plan assets must be named within the bond. This often
leads to confusion when trustees are changed or business policies are rewritten
among various carriers. This reinforces why care and attention to detail must be
taken when making such changes.

In response to corporate malfeasance and improper governance such as Enron
and World Comm, where imprudent and illiquid plan assets were offered as a
self-directed option, plans must now differentiate between qualifying plan assets
and party at interest or hard to value assets. General assets still fall under the same
fidelity bond guidelines, where 10% of the plan value must be covered by the
plan's fidelity bond.

Special class (or nonqualifying) assets would be those that are not regularly
traded on an open exchange or do not have a market established value. Included
would be many hedge funds, private equity funds, non-public initial public offerings (IPOs), and real estate investment trusts (REITS). In the event that nonqualifying assets exceed more than 5% of the total plan value, new regulations
require that either the plan have a full independent audit to verify their value
within the plan, or the fidelity bond be increased to provide coverage equal to the

full value of the special asset.[3] This amount is in addition to the 10% of qualifying assets that must be covered.

Given the reasonable cost associated with most fidelity bonds, the most common approach is to increase the coverage. Nonetheless, it is reasonable to expect that over time, premiums will increase to reflect the fact that both more coverage is being provided and a new asset class (one which by definition is more difficult to value) has begun to be covered.

Transition and Blackout Rules

Recently, several landmark pieces of legislation were passed in response to many of the corporate challenges that arose at or about the turn of the century. Perhaps the most significant of these, if not certainly the most comprehensive, was the Sarbanes-Oxley Act of 2002 (the SOA), enacted on July 30, 2002.

Under Sarbanes-Oxley, ERISA was amended to add a new subsection intended to protect the rights of 401(k) participants as assets were transferred from one investment vehicle to another.[4] Specifically, the new rules state that administrators of individual account plans must provide notice to affected participants and beneficiaries in advance of the commencement of any blackout period. In general, a blackout period includes any period during which the ability of participants to direct or diversify account balances, obtain loans or distributions from the plan will be temporarily suspended, limited or restricted. The most common reasons for imposition of a blackout period include changes in investment options, record keepers, or plan sponsors (including mergers, acquisitions, or spin-offs) that impact the plan coverage of groups of participants.

Subsequent to the issuance of model notices and confirmed regulations, the blackout period is currently defined as 30 days. Thus, under these procedures, plan administrators must post notice 30 days *prior* to any transfer of funds that will limit employee access to their accounts as listed above. Given the fact that these transfers also involve the need for some planning around the switch, the Department of Labor has determined that the notice should contain the name, address and telephone number of a person who can answer questions concerning the blackout period. Initially designed to protect employees from poor communication relating to restricted access to their accounts, provisions such as these can also provide plan participants with the contact information of a responsible party who can handle questions centered around such transfers.

Product Options

Like most financial transactions made today, there is often too much emphasis placed on the bells and whistles of the product at hand, rather than the necessary functions and responsibilities that come with sponsoring a retirement plan. Many insurance and brokerage firms have created sophisticated and flexible products designed to meet the needs of the self-directed 401(k) marketplace. In spite of their size and flexibility, cost and fee sharing arrangements buried deep within these contracts are often difficult to strip out. Many trustees rarely feel satisfied that they have been able to properly fulfill their 404(c) responsibility and thoroughly assess and analyze the fee structure contained within these products.

Clarification must first be made between two distinct, but often blurred functions; asset recordkeeping and plan administration. Recordkeeping involves the maintenance of accounts, the selection of investment options, the allocation of deposits into these options, and the reporting of values to participants on either a daily or quarterly basis. Plan administration involves the compliance, benefit testing, tax reporting and legal maintenance of a qualified plan.

Investment products designed for 401(k) plans come in two basic flavors or service models: full service with all the bells and whistles of turnkey administration, and recordkeeping only. The latter model will require the services of a third party administrator (TPA) as well. Of course, when using a TPA, general investment accounts can be offered as plan investments, but this is very rare within the self-directed plan environment.

Selection of the plan investment product has traditionally been based upon which of the two models is dominant in any one situation. This had led many plan trustees and fiduciaries to make convenient, yet relatively expensive choices. Like most of the investment world, size matters in the land of self-directed 401(k) plans. Thus, the selections available to plan sponsors are far greater as the amount of plan assets and/or number of participants increases.

Fees, Fees, Fees

For purposes of this discussion, we will use asset size as the delineating factor of three broad categories of asset fees. The first will be zero to $1,000,000 in assets; the second will be $1 million to $5 million in plan assets, and the third will be plan assets of $5 million and up. Obviously, in the life span of a 401(k) plan, two or more of the categories may be applicable. Thus, the need to review plan options, and the marketplace in general, is critical.

Micro Plans

In any event, plans with under $1 million in assets are known as micro plans. Often, these are startups or old money purchase or profit sharing plans that are new to the self-directed world. These plans tend to use retail mutual funds or their clones as investment options. Often they are bound together or consolidated by either investment or insurance carriers. Investment companies tend to limit their offerings to their own proprietary or in-house funds, whereas insurance companies combine several fund families into one product. These are bound together by a "wrapper" or recordkeeping platform.

Inherently, there are two types of fees in micro plans. The first are those charges imposed by the investment manager for the underlying funds. Often traditional management and expense charges, these may range from 25 to 125 basis points. Rarely, if ever, do these funds charge an up-front fee, although until recently some did use a B-share or contingent deferred sales charge (CDSC).[5] Often there are 12b-1 or marketing fees that are paid to the record-keeper or plan broker to allow them to service the funds within the plan.

The second fee is often a charge imposed as a consolidator or record-keeper fee. Often called a *wrap fee*, it is an additional asset-based charge added onto the fund investment fee. This fee supports the quarterly statements, on-line fund access, and general trading platform of the 401(k) plan. The size of the fee can vary, often dependent upon the fee structure of the underlying mutual funds. Typical range is from 25 to 100 basis points. When offered by insurance carriers, these wrap type products are technically contained in group annuity contracts. The significance of the group annuity is often a back-end surrender charge imposed on assets leaving the product within a certain number of years.

When offered as either a CDSC or back-end fee, there is no charge imposed on the initial investment of funds. Instead, a fee is assessed if the participant fails to stay in the investment product for a certain number of years. As market pressures increasingly provide micro plans with options historically made available to larger plans, back end charges become less and less prevalent. Many of these funds are benefit sensitive in the sense that terminating or retiring employees are not charged an exit fee, but a fee is charged should the entire plan move to a new investment product.

Finally, many group annuities are able to offer a guaranteed investment account that is quite comparable to an intermediate bond or long term certificate of deposit (CD). These rates tend to be the only option that will *not* decrease in value over time, particularly net of administrative fees. Be advised that one of the most salient questions that can be asked when reviewing a fixed rate account is whether or not the declared rate is net of all wrap or asset fees. The second issue to be determined before placing assets into a fixed or guaranteed account is any liquidity restrictions.

Mid-Range Plans

The next category is the mid-range plans. Like anything that finds itself in the middle of the pack (including children), this group is much more difficult to differentiate and classify. We have selected plans with $1 to $5 million for this grouping, but market forces seem to be narrowing this category even further. So, like middle children, these plans are getting squeezed at both ends of the spectrum.

Mid-range plans tend to offer the same asset categories as micro plans, indeed often offering the same funds line-up as their smaller brethren. What is unique among these plans is that the mutual funds offered are typically priced at the rates offered institutional investors. This makes fund charges lower and more competitively priced. Also, wrap fees tend to be much less prevalent in this market space, and CDSC charges are far less common.

It is also less common to see a clone fund in this size plan category. A clone fund is one where the investments are not made into the actual named mutual fund. Instead, a similar fund is offered which tracks the purchases of main fund. Due to the fact that a clone fund is essentially an approximation of the main mutual fund, this poses two challenges for the plan participant.

The first is that investment performance is never identical to the main fund. The second, and often more challenging problem, is that the share price of the underlying investment does not always equal the share price of the primary fund. In this day and age of on-line money management and downloaded asset tracking, this means that the share price that the participant sees either on-line or in the market section of the newspaper is rarely the same as that reflected by their statement. This, as well as market pressures, have led to an ever-changing definition and categorization of just what constitutes a mid-sized plan.

Large Plans

In the unenviable and broadest possible category of 401(k) investment products, we choose to classify large plans as any that are in excess of $5 million. Notwithstanding the fact that this is an incredibly broad category (given the fact that some large company 401(k) plans have billions of dollars in assets), there are some unique characteristics that apply to the range of investments available to this grouping.

The first and most significant difference is the presence of what are called *open architecture plans*. These plans tend to provide a significant amount of flexibility, and a transparency to the investor (either trustee or plan participant). These funds charge a base fee for their recordkeeping and custodial services. This fee is typically offset by the revenue sharing that most mutual funds provide asset gatherers such as 401(k) product providers. Traditionally, this revenue sharing was rarely disclosed to plan sponsors. In the current climate of increasingly full and fair disclosure, many regulators have begun to signal that these costs and fee arrangements must be disclosed to the consumer.

Additional services provided by an open architecture plan include trustee services, which would accommodate all participant payouts, including loans and terminations, as well as tax withholding and reporting.

In addition, there are many products that feature the services typically found in mid-range plans, with a simply more competitive fee structure that reflects the size of the assets. Often self-directed brokerage accounts are available in these plans. Under these arrangements, participants may buy individual stocks and bonds, rather than be limited to a menu of mutual funds. There is some debate on just how extensive plan investment education must become for such plans. Clearly, Section 404(c) implies a higher standard should be made available.

Investment Preferences: Active vs. Passive

There is a significant debate that has always divided the investment community; it is the clash between two distinct investment styles. The breech has only grown greater over time, and essentially has to do with what value a fund manager can add to one's investment portfolio. There is a significant, and growing, body of evidence that a passive investment, complete with its lower fees and investment costs is a superior asset class to an actively managed fund.[6]

Those who ascribe to active portfolio management feel that a stock picker or market manager adds value to a portfolio. They sometimes justify the higher fees that must be charged to pay an active manager by pointing to market performance that, theoretically, beats the comparable index. However, as the asset category becomes more broad and diversified, this is a harder argument to make. For example, fewer large cap managers are able to consistently beat the S&P 500 over a sustained number of years (net of fees). The success of an active manager tends to be greater in more specialized asset class categories such as small cap stocks or bond funds.

Without interjecting ourselves into the debate, our experience has led us to observe that the larger the plan is in terms of assets, and the more competitive the pressures on keeping fees as low as possible, the more likely a plan is to favor a passive investment style. Being asset allocation junkies and purists, we will still defer to the wisdom of a properly allocated portfolio among a broad range of asset classes over a single fund that boasts it has beaten one particular market index.

Roth 401(k) Feature

The Economic Growth and Tax Reconciliation Relief Act of 2001 created a new 401(k) plan tool scheduled to become available January 1, 2006, known as a Roth 401(k) feature. Participants in plans that offer this feature will be able to designate any or all of their elective deferrals that would otherwise be excludable as *not* being excludable from gross income.

Why would an employee choose to designate an elective deferral as not being excludable from income? Essentially because a Roth 401(k) plan works like a Roth IRA: contributions are made on an after-tax basis, but distributions can be received income tax free. Many participants whose income levels have excluded them from setting up a Roth IRA may be able to obtain the same benefits through a Roth 401(k) plan.

Under regulations proposed in 2005,[7] Roth 401(k) contributions would be subject to another significant advantage: they could be rolled over to a Roth IRA upon retirement or separation from service, meaning that they would not become subject to the lifetime minimum distribution requirements explained in Chapter 6.

The maximum amount that an employee can designate as a Roth 401(k) contribution is the same as the maximum amount of elective deferrals permitted for the tax year (i.e., $14,000 in 2005 for participants in a traditional or safe harbor 401(k) plan who are under age 50). In other words, the participant will be required to reduce the pre-tax elective deferral limit by any amounts being deferred to the Roth portion of the plan. Plans that offer a Roth feature will be required to account for the Roth contributions separately; thus, it may be less feasible for smaller plans.

For income tax purposes, distributions from a Roth 401(k) account will generally be treated very much like distributions from Roth IRAs. The Internal Revenue Code states that *qualified distributions* from a Roth 401(k) account are excluded from gross income.[8] A distribution from a Roth 401(k) account will not be treated as a qualified distribution if it is made within a 5-year "nonexclusion period."[9]

The Roth 401(k) feature is scheduled to take effect beginning January 1, 2006;[10] however, as of the printer date for this book, legislation was pending that would repeal the provision allowing it. Thus, it is unclear whether the provision will take effect as scheduled.

Chapter Endnotes

1. Research Brief *Fundamentals* (Investment Company Institute, June 2004), pp. 1-20.

2. Source: Retirement Planners and Administrators, Falls Church, VA 2003.

3. Labor Reg. §2580.412-15.

4. Sarbanes-Oxley Act, P.L. 107-204, Sec. 306(b)(1).

5. *NASD Special Notice to Members, 02-85,* December 2002 (pp. 927-930), limited the extent to which B shares may be offered by most mutual funds. This was in response to poor understanding by many investors and the recent break-point initiative.

6. See *Does Your Broker Owe you Money,* Daniel R. Solin, (pub. SilverCloud, 2004).

7. See REG-152354-04, proposed amendments to Treas. Regs. §§1.401(k)-1 to 1.401(k)-6; 1.401(m)-1 to 1.401(m)-5, 70 Fed. Reg. 10062 (March 2, 2005).

8. "Qualified distribution" for this purpose, means a distribution made after the 5-taxable-year period beginning with the tax year of the contribution, provided the distribution meets one of three requirements: (1) it is made on or after the individual reaches age 59½, (2) it is made to a beneficiary or the individual's estate after death, *or* (3) it is attributable to the individual being disabled. The term does not include any distributions of excess deferrals or excess contributions, nor income on them. IRC Sec. 402A(d)(2)(C).

9. The 5-year nonexclusion period begins with: (a) the first taxable year the individual made a designated Roth contribution to any designated Roth account established for him under the same retirement plan, *or* (b) if a rollover contribution was made to the designated Roth account from another designated Roth account, the first year which the individual made a Roth contribution to the previous account. See IRC Sec. 402A(d)(2)(B).

10. EGTRRA 2001 (P.L. 107-16), Sec. 617(a).

Chapter 9

Life Insurance Anyone?

One of the least utilized and often misunderstood features of most qualified plans is the ability to add a life insurance component as part of the benefit. This is available in both defined benefit and defined contribution plans, although with a slightly different set of rules and regulations for each. The opportunity to purchase a policy must be drafted into the plan trust document, and, of course, the trustees must be confident that the provision will be accepted and properly utilized by the participants.

In general, Treasury regulations require that life insurance, if included as a part of the plan, must be incidental in nature. For defined contribution plans, IRS guidance defines this incidental limit as a percentage of the actual deposit. Before explaining these rules, we will spend a few moments detailing the reasons why one would want to consider using life insurance within a retirement plan.

By definition, retirement programs are long-term assets. As such, much of the planning associated with them tends to include long range planning as well. Quite simply, for those participants who have a need to provide for someone financially in the event of their death, life insurance may be the best way to fulfill that need. The decision whether or not to place that coverage into a qualified plan is based upon a variety of factors, but is certainly worthy of analysis.

The largest single reason to place insurance into a retirement plan is the fact that premiums become immediately tax deductible. Whether new deposits are utilized to pay premiums, or funds contained within existing account balances are used, the basic net effect is that pre-tax dollars have gone into fulfilling the obligations. Subject to certain guidelines, the net proceeds may also be payable to beneficiaries on a pre-tax basis as well.

Potential obstacles include the added complexity of offering insurance as an investment option, cumbersome portability given the fact that policies *may not* be rolled into an IRA (for terminees and retirees), and underwriting challenges, which may delay the allocation of funds into investment choices. More on that later, but first some detail on the placement of policies and some of the guidelines limiting how much insurance may be purchased.

How it Works

In a defined contribution plan, a life policy simply becomes an additional asset owned by the trust. Accordingly, it may either be self-directed by the participant, in which case it is directly allocated to that person's account, or it may be a part of the general plan assets. If the policy has a cash value associated with it, that amount would be added to the account balance of the participant. The payment of premiums is debited against the account balance of the participant (subject to certain limitations detailed below).

The policy series used must be unisex as required by the Retirement Equity Act of 1984.[1] The participant is free to choose his or her beneficiary as with most life policies. Typically, the incidents of ownership that reflect this control dictate that the policy be included in the participant's estate. Under a concept developed by attorney Andrew Fair, a planning technique called the subtrust has been developed that effectively establishes an irrevocable insurance trust within a qualified plan. Neither approved, nor disapproved by the Internal Revenue Service, the concept remains somewhat controversial, although also an ingenious technique.[2]

Insurance Limits

For purposes of a defined benefit program, the maximum allowable death benefit is a function or multiple of the projected monthly benefit being funded for under the plan. Typically restricted to a limit of 100 times the monthly benefit, this is a fairly simple guideline. Of course, a more complicated version is available, and may result in a higher benefit.

For purposes of an overall limitation, Revenue Ruling 74-307[3] imposes a general limitation that roughly half of the annual cost to fund benefits may be allocated to funding the death benefit. Based upon the fact that the annual cost to fund a defined benefit is based upon a presumed return on future assets, the presence of a permanent life policy adds to the deductible cost. Thus, in certain situations, this may be an advantage for older, more highly compensated employees, who may also tend to be owners.

For the defined contribution plan, which is more germane to our 401(k) discussion, the limitation is a function of the annual cost or premium for coverage. The basic rule is that 50% of annual deposits may be used to purchase whole life coverage, and 25% of annual deposits may be used for either term or universal life insurance.[4] This limit is calculated annually, and quite simply based upon the annual contribution allocated to each participant.

> *Example 1:* Jo is a participant in a 401(k) plan. She defers $10,000 per year and her employer matches 25 cents per dollar deferred. In addition, there is a profit sharing deposit, which was an additional contribution of $5,000 for the year; thus, her total deposit is $17,500. In turn, she may allocate $8,750 towards a whole life policy or $4,375 towards term or universal life coverage. This dollar limit may not be exceeded should the insurance carrier charge her an additional premium due to her underwriting classification or general insurability.

These insurance limits for defined contribution plans are part of a cumulative test. Thus, if a participant opts to use the allocation starting in the second year, the unused limit from the prior year may be added to the limit for this current year. Of course, it is important to build some flexibility into the policy design in such a circumstance, as the deposit may again revert back to a smaller (either 50% or 25%) amount of next year's deposit.

Another word of caution here; in the event that one of the contribution elements changes, the policy must have additional flexibility. For example, due to problems with ADP testing (see Chapter 4), some participants may not be able to defer as much as they would like. Alternatively, profit sharing deposits may be reduced, or matching deposits limited. For this reason, life insurance was more commonly offered in conjunction with money purchase plans, where the trust document calls for a set percentage of pay to be deposited annually.

Fortunately for the profit sharing plan (PSP) sponsor, there is a second set of rules, called seasoned money rules, which provide PSP participants with the ability to match the flexibility of a profit sharing structure with the inflexibility of some life products. For purposes of profit sharing accounts that allow participants to exercise self-direction from a group of investments, one of these elections may be a life insurance policy. Once account balances have remained in the plan for more than two years, all of these assets may be applied to the purchase of a policy. Similarly, if an employee has been a plan participant for five or more years, his or her entire balance may be allocated to a life policy.

The existence of this regulation does not immediately imply that participants *should* allocate every penny in their account balance to the purchase of life insurance. But in certain select circumstances, where the value of plan account balance is not a meaningful part of the individual's retirement income, this might be a source of dollars for life insurance.

Ancillary Costs – Imputed Income

When a qualified plan purchases insurance on the life of the participant, the participant must pay income taxes on the economic value of the death benefit protection.[5] The economic value is equal to the pure term cost of the insurance benefit provided.[6] If the policy insures the life of the participant only, the taxable amount is measured either under the Table 2001 (formerly P.S. 58 table for single life coverage and P.S. 38 for second to die coverage) or the yearly renewable term rate charged by the insurance company for policies issued by the same carrier and available to the same class of insured. Additionally, the amount included in income by the participant is considered to be his or her basis in the policy.[7] Some third party administrators or trustees will keep track of these amounts, but the participant is ultimately responsible for reporting the appropriate basis under the plan.

In exchange for the imputed income recognized by the participant, the death proceeds receive special tax treatment once paid. The net amount at risk under the policy (death benefit minus cash value) is paid income tax free to the beneficiary. This is a significant advantage, particularly should there be a claim in the early years of the policy or in the event that a low cash value secondary guarantee policy is utilized. Purely from a return on investment point of view, this leverage helps to make the death proceeds of a policy an extremely competitive investment (albeit one that comes at a high price for the insured).

Transfer of Policies

Once a policy is purchased by using plan assets, a participant may wish to transfer it out of the plan and into a trust or some other form of ownership. One of the disadvantages of a life policy contained within a qualified plan trust is that such transfers can be cumbersome. The first challenge is to properly value the policy. Until recently, IRS communication on the proper valuation of a policy being transferred from a retirement plan was murky, at best.

Of late, this has become a hot issue, as companies created policies that were designed to suppress the cash value and then, after being transferred from the plan, grow at an accelerated rate. Another variation has been the practice of aggressively funding a policy and after transfer, reducing the death benefit. The ensuing policy will experience a reduction in expenses, and the cash value will begin to grow at an incrementally faster rate.

In 2004 the Service defined a safe harbor method of policy valuation[8] which was intended to clarify the situation. Unfortunately, the safe harbor definition of policy valuation created even further confusion, and the professional community remained in a state of flux regarding proper policy valuation. The guidance was revised in April, 2005.

Under the 2005 guidance, the fair market value of a life insurance contract is generally the greater of (1) the interpolated terminal reserve (plus any unearned premiums, and a pro rata portion of dividends), or (2) the product of the "PERC amount" (premiums, earnings, and reasonable charges) and the applicable "Average Surrender Factor."[9]

Prohibited Transaction Issues

The next step associated with a policy transfer is to carefully navigate the transaction around a set of carefully constructed prohibited transaction rules. Both ERISA and the Revenue Code prohibit certain transactions between the qualified plan and particular individuals. In the event of a prohibited transaction, penalty taxes of up to 100 percent of the amount involved can be levied against the parties engaging in the transaction. A prohibited transaction occurs when the qualified plan and a "party in interest" engage in any of the following transactions:

1. The sale, leasing, or exchange of any property;

2. A loan or extension of credit;

3. The furnishing of goods, services, or facilities for a fee or remuneration;

4.   A transfer of plan assets, or the use of plan assets; and

5.   An acquisition of employer securities or employer real property above
     the limits allowed by law.[10]

The list of individuals or entities who may be a party in interest includes the
employer, the participant, a fiduciary to the plan, a relative of any of the above,
and a corporation or other entity (trust, estate, partnership) owned more than
50% by any of the above.

How then, may an existing policy be sold into or out of a qualified plan? In a
word, carefully. The Service has also granted a class exemption from the prohibited transaction rules for certain transfers of policies from a plan, provided special requirements are met. In order to qualify for the exemption, the transaction
must comply with the following:

1.   The plan document must allow for the purchase of the policy.

2.   The plan cannot pay more for the policy than the cash surrender
     value. If the participant's plan account balance is less than the surren-
     der value of the policy, the purchase price cannot exceed the plan bal-
     ance via loan or an indenture agreement.

3.   The policy being purchased by the plan cannot have any outstanding
     loans.[11]

Similarly, there are specific steps that must be followed when engaging in the
sale of a policy from a plan. These include:

1.   The policy must first be offered to the participant before being sold to
     any other permitted purchasers.

2.   If the participant does not wish to purchase the policy, this must be
     noted in writing to the plan, and written authorization given to allow
     someone else to purchase the policy.

3.   If the participant does not wish to purchase the policy, it can be sold
     to a relative of the participant (if the relative is a beneficiary under
     the contract), the employer of the participant, or another qualified
     plan.

4.   The policy, but for the sale, would be surrendered by the plan.

5.   The plan must receive, as payment, an amount equal to the amount the plan would have received if the policy were surrendered.[12]

Even given the new finalized definition of fair market value defined above, the result of violating this valuation may clearly be classification as a prohibited transaction. Therefore, special care must be exercised to follow the IRS guidelines when transferring a policy.

In a critical proclamation, the Department of Labor stated that a plan could sell a life insurance policy to multiple parties as long as all of the parties are beneficiaries of the policy, either directly or in trust.[13] In addition, the 1998 advisory opinion concluded that the sale of a second-to-die contract would also qualify under the prohibited transaction exemption as long as all of the other requirements for exemption are met.

Distribution Planning Issues

Often, participants in retirement plans experience a wonderful and often unanticipated set of problems. The funds contained in their retirement accounts, although intended to be the mainstay of their income during retirement, become somewhat inconsequential in the larger scheme of things. This can occur particularly with entrepreneurs and plan sponsors who have seen their other assets grow. Assets such as home(s), the family business, stock portfolios, etc., have grown to amounts that suddenly reduces the importance, if not the necessity, of using plan account values as a source of retirement income.

When faced with such an enviable set of problems, many plan participants begin to look to the qualified plan as a source of life insurance funding. Under the right circumstances, as detailed in Chapter 6, the opportunity can exist to pass these assets favorably to future generations *and* preserve their tax deferred growth. At this stage, life insurance, purchased within or outside of the qualified plan, can provide the liquidity necessary to pay the estate taxes that are due as these assets are transferred via the stretch out technique.

Survivorship Insurance

Often a participant opts to utilize a second to die or survivorship policy to provide the liquidity at a time when estate taxes become due. The use of a retirement plan account as a source of pre-tax premiums may often help enhance the appeal of such a solution. In addition to the qualified pension plan rules regarding purchases of second-to-die coverage, there are several important planning issues to consider when determining who should be beneficiary of the policy. Depending on whether the participant or non-participant spouse dies first, the income and estate tax consequences will vary upon distribution of the policy from the plan.

If the Participant Dies First

If the participant dies first, only the cash surrender value, as part of the participant's account value, is includable in the estate (this is because no death proceeds are payable until the second of both insureds dies). However, if the surviving spouse is the beneficiary of the decedent's plan account, the cash value of the policy passing to the non-participant spouse will be eligible for the unlimited marital deduction. Thus, no estate tax would be payable.

In the event that the surviving spouse dies while still owning the policy, the value of the death proceeds will clearly be included in his or her estate. Once the policy is distributed to the surviving spouse, the spouse can gift the policy to an irrevocable life insurance trust (ILIT) to remove the policy from the taxable estate. Of course, such a gift may be subject to gift taxes in and of itself. In either event, the 3-year rule would apply; should the spouse die within three years of transfer, the policy will be includible in his or her taxable estate. Should the spouse survive three years, the proceeds will be assured exclusion from the estate.

When distributing the policy to the surviving spouse following the participant's death, the policy fair market value (as defined in the 2005 guidance described above) will be subject to income tax at the surviving spouse's income tax rate. The balance of any remaining qualified plan balance can be rolled over to the surviving spouse's own IRA, thus deferring immediate income tax on the rest of the plan distribution. But since life insurance may not be placed into an IRA, the distributed policy may not be rolled over to the surviving spouse's IRA.

Should the participant so desire, the policy may be transferred directly to an irrevocable life insurance trust (ILIT) by naming that trust as the beneficiary of the plan for an amount equal to the value of the policy. Another viable option may be to have the surviving spouse disclaim the policy; the policy would then pass to the contingent beneficiary which could be the ILIT. Either of these techniques would avoid potential inclusion in the surviving spouse's estate (in addition to the 3-year inclusion period) because the surviving spouse never held any incidents of ownership over the policy.

If the Nonparticipant Spouse Dies First

In the event that the nonparticipant spouse is the first to die, the participant is best served to remove the policy itself as a distribution from the plan, and then gift it to an ILIT. The participant would pay income tax if the policy is distributed (and the 10% penalty tax if under age 59½), or as detailed below, the ILIT could purchase the policy from the plan. Provided that the participant lives three years beyond the transfer, the policy proceeds will not be included in the participant's estate.

The transfer to the ILIT is a gift for transfer tax purposes. Again, caution must be taken to ensure that the proper value is ascribed to the policy at each step along the way under the guidance described earlier in this chapter.

Purchasing the Policy from the Plan

A purchase of the policy from the plan may be preferable to taking a taxable distribution of the policy. This alternative should allow the parties to avoid any income or early distribution tax and leaves assets in the plan that can be used for retirement benefits. However, there are three challenges that must be met for the purchase of the policy to work.

1. The purchaser must have the liquidity to purchase the policy from the plan.

2. The purchase must not be deemed a prohibited transaction.

3. The purchase must avoid the transfer-for-value rules.

If these three barriers can be avoided, then often the purchase of a policy is the most logical and efficient approach.

The first challenge is sufficient cash flow. Does the potential purchaser (be it a trust or a child) have the funds to purchase the policy? In order to avoid a prohibited transaction, the purchaser must pay at least the fair market value of the policy, so the purchaser must have the necessary liquidity or access to a credit facility that will provide the funds required to make the purchase.

In order to purchase the policy without creating a prohibited transaction, the steps outlined earlier in this chapter must be carefully followed. Particular attention should be focused on following the procedures detailed in PTE 92-6.[14] As with the taxable distribution method, the purchase of a policy may be done by the participant and then transferred to an ILIT. Again, the 3-year rule becomes a concern, as do the liquidity issues and possible gift taxes associated with such a transaction.

Another option is to allow the participant's irrevocable trust or a child to purchase the policy from the plan. Use of this method should avoid the 3-year rule, provided that the transfer is for full and adequate consideration.[15] Once again, if a trust or child is going to purchase the policy instead of the participant, the participant can certainly gift the needed funds to the child or trust. Often, we have found that with some foresight, the unified credit of the presumably deceased non-participant spouse can also be an excellent source of funds. Care must therefore be given, when drafting the credit shelter trust, to provide the trustees the necessary powers to allow for the purchase of a life insurance policy.

Care must be taken at this stage to ensure that if the policy is purchased by any sort of trust, that the ultimate beneficiary of that trust is a class which is provided exemption under the prohibited transaction rules.

Although we have outlined the steps to allow the policy purchase to avoid inclusion in the estate, there is one final pitfall. The third obstacle—the transfer-for value rules—may be the most dangerous of the three listed above.[16] Truly, it is the least heeded and most often disregarded. When a policy is transferred for valuable consideration, the death benefit becomes income taxable to the extent it exceeds the purchaser's basis in the contract (this is true for term as well as permanent policies). Fortunately, there are several exceptions to the transfer-for-value rule. If the transfer is to a person or entity falls under one of these exceptions, the death benefit can be paid income tax free. The excepted parties are:

1.   The insured,

2.   A partner of the insured,

3.   A partnership in which the insured is a partner, or

4.   A corporation in which the insured is an officer or shareholder.

In order to avoid the adverse tax consequences of a transfer for value, a bona fide partnership arrangement could be established to take advantage of the partnership exception to the transfer-for-value rule.[17] The child, as a partner of the insured in a bona fide partnership, may purchase the policy from the plan trust as an exception to the transfer-for-value rule. It should be noted that as long as parent and child are partners in *any* venture, not just one involving the transaction, the exception will apply.

If a trust is the intended purchaser, there are two potential exceptions to the transfer-for-value rule available. One, the trust could become a bona fide partner in the same manner as could a child. Secondly, if the trust is a grantor trust for income tax purposes, then the exception for transfers to the insured would apply.

Summary

The use of untaxed dollars may be one of the most powerful concepts to be applied to the purchase of a life insurance policy. And, the application of such a technique may create even further advantages for those in need of significant liquidity at death. Clearly, though, it is not for the faint of heart, or those uneducated in the nuances and intricacies of such a transaction.

Chapter Endnotes

1. Under the Retirement Equity Act of 1984, it is unlawful to distinguish between rates charged by gender. In certain select circumstances, with trustee authorization and recognition by the participant, sex specific rates may be used.

2. *See generally*, Andrew Fair, Guardian Life Ins. Co. of Amercia, Pub. 1261, *The Qualified Plan As An Estate Planning Tool - Advanced Techniques Using Life Insurance* (Dec. 1992).

3. Rev. Rul. 74-307, 1974-2 CB 126.

4. There has been some debate on which limit should be applied to universal life policies, but in Field Service Advice (FSA) 1999-633, the IRS clarified that universal life policies are subject to the 25% limitation.

5. Treas. Reg. §1.72-16(b).

6. IRC Sec. 72(m)(3)(b).

7. See IRC Sec. 72(m).

8. Rev Proc 2004-16 established interim rules whereby a policy's fair market value is defined as the total premiums paid plus an appropriate credit for policy earnings, minus reasonable mortality and expenses actually charged.

9. See Rev. Proc. 2005-25, 2005-17 IRB 962, superseding Rev. Proc. 2004-16, 2004-10 IRB 559.

10. ERISA Sec. 406(a)(1); IRC Sec. 4975.

11. DOL Prohibited Transaction Exemption (PTE) 92-5, 57 Fed. Reg. 5019 (February 11, 1992).

12. DOL Prohibited Transaction Exemption (PTE) 92-6, 57 Fed. Reg. 5189 (February 12, 1992).

13. DOL Advisory Opinion 98-07A.

14. See text accompanying footnote 12, above.

15. This must be done in accordance with the process detailed in Section 2035.

16. IRC Sec. 101(a)(2).

17. It is clear that the partnership must be a legitimate entity properly established under federal and state laws. The IRS has described a set of steps that may preserve the transfer for value exception. See PLR 200111038.

Chapter 10

Running an Enrollment Meeting

A properly designed and well functioning 401(k) plan is like a well-balanced stool built upon three legs; the investment product leg, the third party administrative leg, and the plan communication leg. All three legs must be equally competent and capable, but the communication leg is the one that may well play the largest part in determining the success of the plan as determined by those with the most say, the plan participants.

Often plan sponsors and many plan administrators lose sight of the employee aspect of the employee benefit world. Retirement plans, in particular, are programs designed with the initial intention of being utilized and accepted by employees. This acceptance should span income levels and departments, job tenure and overall job title. This is particularly true for employee-driven programs like 401(k) plans. In the current environment, many employees' only form of long-term savings is through their employer-sponsored retirement plan. All the more reason why these programs, their rules, features and benefits need to be properly communicated in as simple and accurate a manner as is possible.

Ideally, our preference is to hold individual enrollment sessions where we meet live in front of those eligible for the plan. This tends to be practical with groups offering participation to less than 500 people. The primary objective of each enrollment session is to provide a basic or cursory understanding of the plan. Our preference is to run group meetings, generally with a range of 10-40 people included. This session is intended to accomplish a few things, which will be detailed below. We tend to keep this session about 20-30 minutes in length – no more. In a group setting, specific action steps should be reviewed clearly and succinctly.

During the session we encourage questions, commenting that in all probability, other share the same or similar concerns. Following the group session, we make ourselves available to answer simplified specific questions that typically mean spending ten minutes with anyone who sticks around. In addition, we always make ourselves available to review the extent to which this plan can be integrated into their personal planning. This may require a more detailed financial planning session, which we are happy to schedule separately.

This has also proven to be one of the best training opportunities for developing young talent within our organization. The opportunity to meet with and plan for a solid core of prospects in their place of work has been a key in developing our planning practice further. Conversely, the planner is already being compensated for his or her own time to review the plan details with the participant. As such, there is less sales pressure placed on either the planner or the prospect, and the entire process can be carried out in a more consultative manner.

Meeting Objectives

The number one purpose of the enrollment meeting is to review and detail the basic plan details. The goal is to explain what the plan is, who is eligible, the basic rules and limits, etc. We have found that a simple question and answer format works best here. A sample format that we like to use is shown in Figure 10.1.

The top features are reviewed, with simple (non-actuarial) answers listed. Effort is made to highlight only the most basic of topics. Detail and potential exceptions to the rules are left for a separate session, or handled in the question and answer period. In addition, they will also be covered in the summary plan description (SPD). Although referenced, investment details are typically handled in a separate document

Once of the most central distinctions that we feel should be made at an enrollment meeting is a word or two on the flow of dollars involved and a little bit about the tax theory behind a qualified plan. We start by mentioning that a qualified plan may well be the best place to save funds on a long-term basis. It is not a solid place to save for shorter-term needs such as funding education, vacations, or the purchase of a new car. Furthermore, what the term "qualified" implies is that the plan has followed several very basic IRS rules and therefore qualifies for a tax deduction.

FIGURE 10.1

SAMPLE CLIENT 401(k) Plan

EFFECTIVE DATE: January 1, 2005

ENTRY DATES: January 1st & July 1st

RE-ENROLLMENT DATES: January 1st
July 1st

VALUATION DATE: December 31st

WHEN CAN I BECOME A MEMBER? You will be eligible for Plan participation if you have worked for SAMPLE CLIENT for one year as of any subsequent entry date and have attained age 21.

EMPLOYEE CONTRIBUTIONS: You have the option to defer a percentage of your salary up to the annual maximum determined by the Treasury Department each year ($14,000 in 2005). You may also make catch up deposits of $4,000 in 2005 if you have attained 50 by December 31, 2005.

SAMPLE CLIENT will put away a minimum of 3% of pay for all eligible employees, whether you make salary deferrals or not. From time to time, SAMPLE CLIENT may choose to match your deferrals or make additional profit sharing deposits. This will be declared and communicated by the firm on an annual basis.

WHAT HAPPENS IF I LEAVE THE COMPANY? You are always fully vested in your own deferrals, the fixed 3% deposit, and their earnings. Should you leave the firm, you will vest in company deposits, and their growth, as per the following schedule :

YEARS OF SERVICE	VESTED PERCENT
1 year	0%
2 years	20%
3 years	40%
4 years	60%
5 years	80%
6 years	100%

SAMPLE CLIENT 401(k) Plan

WHAT ARE MY OPTIONS AT RETIREMENT? You may receive your benefit from the Plan in the form of a Lump Sum Distribution or an Annuity may be purchased on your behalf. This annuity will allow for you to receive a fixed monthly benefit payable for the remainder of you life of the life of you and your spouse.

HOW ARE DEFERRALS INVESTED? You will have the option of selecting from the funds offered within the SAMPLE FAVORITE PRODUCT program. Details on these funds, their performance, and restrictions, will be reviewed in a separate summary.

FIGURE 10.1 (cont'd)

WHAT HAPPENS IF I DIE PRIOR TO RETIREMENT? If you die before you retire or terminate your services with the Plan Sponsor, your beneficiary will receive the full value of your account balance.

WHAT HAPPENS IF I BECOME DISABLED PRIOR TO RETIREMENT? If you are totally and permanently disabled and unable to work, you will vest 100% in your match account.

THE TRUST FUND: The Company puts the money for the pension benefits into a trust fund. The money can only be used for the benefit of the employees of the Company and the Company cannot use the funds for any other purpose. The status of the fund is reported to the Federal Government annually.

This is a brief explanation of your benefits under the SAMPLE CLIENT 401(k) Plan. The provision of the trust document will be subject to an IRS final review.

Details, Details

Now, precisely how does that tax deduction work? When it comes to employee deferrals, employers receive the same tax treatment that they would receive if the funds were paid out as compensation. Meanwhile, the employee is spared from having to pay income tax on the funds deferred. Under the rules of constructive receipt, if you have unfettered access to funds, they are generally included in your taxable income. However, with regard to a 401(k) plan, taxation of the employee is deferred because a third entity other than the employee or employer holds on to the funds. This entity is the pension trust account.

The pension trust account is a separate legal entity that is obliged to file its own tax return (Form 5500—see Chapter 11), has its own set of operating instructions (detailed in the trust document), and even has its own tax identification number. This separate entity is where their salary deferral funds reside. In a technical sense, it means that the funds no longer belong to the employer, *and* the employee does not yet have control of the funds. They are held by the plan, on behalf of the employee. This is a critical concept to communicate, because it will invariably come into play at some point in the future when participants demand access to "their money" while still employed by the sponsoring firm.

Timing of Deposits

One of the questions most commonly asked by plan administrators is when do these deferrals have to be submitted to the investment vehicle chosen for the plan. Typically confronting issues of administrative burden, and sometimes looking to maximize corporate float and liquidity, the question is actually a good one, as there is no true definitive response.

Regulations require that salary deferrals become "plan assets" as of the earliest date by which these assets can be reasonably segregated from general assets of the sponsoring firm.[1] Try having a discussion with a roomful of human resource professionals on how to properly define reasonable.... Issues such as taking time to confirm the accuracy of payroll withdrawals and deposit allocations, complications for firms with multiple locations and payrolls, vacations or sick leave of those responsible for carrying out the task, and so on have become a matter of both employee/employer debate as well as coming within the purview of the courts.

Regulations[2] settle the outside range of the debate, stating in no uncertain terms that deposits must be made no later than:

(a) in the case of amounts withheld by an employer from a participant's wages: the 15th business day of the month following the month in which such amounts would otherwise have been payable to the participant in cash, *or*

(b) in the case of amounts that a participant or beneficiary pays to an employer (such as loan repayments) the 15th business day of the month following the month in which the participant contribution amounts are received by the employer.

The significance of when funds become plan assets rather than corporate assets can been seen in a 2002 case from the Fifth Circuit court.[3] The court ruled that in the strictest sense, plan contributions deducted from employee paychecks are plan assets even before they are actually delivered to the plans. A concurring opinion specified that, under Labor Reg. §2510.3-102(a), employee plan contributions made through payroll deductions become plan assets *immediately*. Under this interpretation, companies have a grace period before having to segregate the deductions from their general accounts—but that does not mean that there is a delay before the payroll deductions become plan assets.

Plan Investments

As detailed in Chapter 7, our opinion of prudent investing is squarely centered on asset allocation. Rather than trying to turn each potential participant into a Chartered Financial Analyst, we attempt to broadly defined asset allocation, detail the major asset classes represented in the plan's current lineup, and introduce the basic rules of risk and reward.

We will also introduce whatever tool is being used to measure risk tolerance. This has already been described in Chapter 7, but there are many assessment tools from which to choose. This step should not be skipped, although other methods for discussing and measuring risk are certainly acceptable.

Plan Enrollment Forms

So how do I know what you want to do, unless you tell me? Just as plan communication from trustee and enroller to plan participant is critical, so is the communication from the participant back to the plan administrators. To run a successful enrollment meeting, the key becomes how and when you ask the participant to respond with some direction.

First things first. The "how" part is as varied as the possible elections that the participant can make. Basic issues include personal and employment data of the participant, including legal name, address, and employee identification or Social Security number (more firms seem to be using internal identification numbers as concerns for privacy and protection of credit identity grows). Critical dates such as date of hire and date of birth must be checked, as they can have an impact on plan eligibility and certain other features.

Next comes the central election. All employees must complete a form because we prefer to have an indication from all eligible employees as to whether they want to participate. In essence, this confirms that they have been presented their options, and even if they have opt *not* to enter the plan, they need to state so. Should they opt to join the plan, they then must declare what percentage they wish to defer, preferably expressed as a percentage of pay (although fixed dollar amounts are acceptable).

Last but not least, they must pick their investment options. The details associated with this decision have already been reviewed. Bear in mind that if a plan has a safe harbor or basic profit sharing provision, and offers this to all eligible employees, all must select an investment allocation. This is true even if they opt *not* to make deferrals into the plan.

After all these technical details have been resolved, here comes the really tough question – "When do you need these back?" Our preferred answer is anywhere from seven to ten days. There is no need to belabor the issue. Although many are sometimes thrown into fits of a cold sweat when faced with the awesome responsibility of making such life altering decisions, they will eventually have to bite the bullet and choose to do something.

A good enroller will explain that laggards will slow the entire process down for others and that proper administration can commence only after all those who are eligible have made some sort of reply.

Negative Elections

In response to a growing desire to increase participation, the DOL has ruled on and created a set of procedures that allow for what is known as a negative election[4] (also known as "automatic enrollment"). What this provision allows is essentially a default decision of participation for any participant who does not *elect out* of being in the plan. Typically, there is some basic deferral amount selected (usually 3%) and some moderate asset allocation. This allows the trustee to enroll *all* eligible employees unless they specifically opt out of the program. Thus, even the folks who rarely pay attention to the bulletin board in the company lunchroom will eventually raise an eyebrow when their next few paychecks are lower.

A sample enrollment form is shown in Figure 10.2. This is an area where enroller and trustee preference has a fair amount of leeway. Be sure to hit the main points that we have reviewed, and encourage those eligible to reply in a timely manner.

Beneficiary Designations

So who gets to keep all these funds if the participant is not lucky enough to enjoy them? Believe it or not, this has been one of the more vigorously and hotly debated topics of qualified plans. To settle matters, and "keep the peace," the answer has actually been legislated by Congress in one of the many tax bills that seemed to reform qualified plans every year or so in the 1980s.[5]

By default, the beneficiary of all qualified plan account balances, for all married participants, is automatically their spouse. Any decision to change that beneficiary to name anyone else, must be authorized via signature of the spouse (which in turn must also be notarized, or witnessed by a plan administrator).

FIGURE 10.2

Participant Enrollment Form

Participant Name:

Address:

City:	State:	Zip Code:

Social Security Number: - -	Sex: M ❑ F ❑ (check one)

Date of Birth: /   /   Date of Hire: /   /   Date of Rehire: /   /   (if applicable)

Participation Election

❑ In accordance with the provisions of the Plan, I elect to contribute _____% of my salary
per pay period to the Plan. I understand that I may change, suspend, and resume contributions at such times as outlined in the plan.

❑ In accordance with the provisions of the Plan, I elect to change my contribution to
_____% per pay period to the Plan. I understand that I may change, suspend, and
resume contributions at such times as outlined in the plan.

❑ I elect not to participate at this time.

Investment Selection

Please indicate below how you would like to have your contributions invested. Make sure
the total of all percentages adds up to 100%.

Percent	Name of Fund	Asset Class
_____%	Your Favorite Money Market	Stability of Principal
_____%	Your Favorite Total Return Fund	Interm. Term Corp. Bond
_____%	Your Favorite High Yield Corp Bond	High Yield Bond
_____%	Your Favorite GNMA	Interm. Government
_____%	Your Favorite Long-Tm US Treasury	Long Government
_____%	Your Favorite Short-Tm Treasury	Short Government
_____%	Your Favorite Wellington	Moderate Allocation
_____%	Your Favorite 500 Index	Large Cap Blend
_____%	Your Favorite Growth	Large Cap Growth
_____%	Your Favorite Value	Large Cap Value
_____%	Your Favorite Total Stock Market Index	Large Cap Blend
_____%	Your Favorite Mid-Cap Index	Mid Cap Blend
_____%	Your Favorite Strategic Equity	Mid Cap Blend
_____%	Your Favorite Small-Cap Index	Small Cap Blend
_____%	Your Favorite Small Cap Growth	Small Cap Growth
_____%	Your Favorite International Stock Index	Foreign Large Cap Blend
_____%	Your Favorite Index	Specialty Real Estate
_____%	Your Favorite Science & Technology	Specialty Technology
100%		

EMPLOYEE SIGNATURE _____   Date _____

EMPLOYER SIGNATURE _____   Date _____

FIGURE 10.3

Beneficiary Designation Form

Employer Name:_____ Contract Number: _____

Employee: _____ Social Security No: _____

Check a box below and complete appropriate section.

❑ 1) I am NOT MARRIED and designate the following persons(s) to receive any death benefits. I understand if I marry, the designation becomes void one year after my marriage.

SS#	Name	Relationship	Address	Amount/%

❑ 2) I am MARRIED and designate my spouse named below to receive ALL death benefits from the Plan.

Spouse's Name	Spouse's Address

If my spouse is not living, then pay death benefits to:

SS#	Name	Relationship	Address	Amount/%

❑ 3) I am MARRIED and designate the following person(s) to receive death benefits from the Plan.

SS#	Name	Relationship	Address	Amount/%

Spouse consent (Required for #3 above):
I consent to this designation, which eliminates all, or part of the benefits (Qualified Joint and Survivor and Qualified Pre-Retirement Survivor benefits) otherwise payable to me from the plan if my spouse dies.

Spouse'e Signature	Date

❑ (Check if Applicable)
I certify that my spouse cannot be located to sign this Spouse's consent. I will notify my Employer if my spouse is located.

Plan Representative Signature (witness)   Date

Notary Public (if not witnessed by Plan Representative)   Date

Subscribe and sworn before me this _____ day of _____19_____

This designation revokes all prior designations made under the plan.

Employee Signature   Date

Employer Signature   Date

Note that for purposes of this provision, "separated but not legally divorced" still means "married." In addition, if someone is single when completing their plan paperwork, and later becomes married, their spouse automatically becomes their beneficiary from that point on.

It should be noted that this provision transcends a prenuptial agreement. In fact, an attorney we work with tells the story of a second marriage with kids and significant assets involved on one side of the relationship. It appears that on the way from the ceremony to the wedding reception, the more affluent of the two stopped the limo until their new "better half" signed the waiver of benefits. It is not clear whether the limo driver was a notary – but the case proves our point of how contested beneficiary designations can be.

For illustration, a copy of a beneficiary designation form is shown in Figure 10.3.

Scalability

A final word about size and scope. As mentioned, most of our clients range in number of employees from one to 500. These personalized techniques work fine in a marketplace this size. Once a firm exceeds this basic range, such enrollment methods can often become unruly. Nonetheless, the same basic data can be communicated, albeit in a slightly different manner.

Modern tools such as electronic enrollment, webinars, video conferencing or custom made videotapes can all be excellent means by which the message can then be spread. The most critical elements of these efforts are that the employees understand the basic plan provisions, get some form of appropriate investment education, and be clearly told what decisions they have to make and by what date. Being flexible and creative with such matters can be one of the most telling signs of experience and professionalism that a benefits specialist can exhibit.

Chapter Endnotes

1. "Plan assets" include the amounts (other than union dues) of participant contributions to the plan as of the earliest date on which the contributions can reasonably be segregated from the employer's general assets. This rule applies to participant contributions as:

    ... payments by a participant or beneficiary to an employer, or

    ... amounts withheld by an employer from a participant's wages.

    Labor Reg. §2510.3-102(a).

2. See Labor Reg. §2510.3-102.

3. *Bannistor v. Ullman,* 287 F.3d 394, 27 EBC 2249 (5th Cir. 2002).

4. Negative elections were first approved by the IRS in 1998, then expanded in later pronouncements. See Rev. Rul. 98-30, 1998-1 CB 1273; Rev. Rul. 2000-8, 2000-1 CB 617; Treas. Reg. §1.401(k)-1(g)(3).

5. See Retirement Equity Act of 1984, P.L. 98-397.

Chapter 11

Filing and Related Requirements

All qualified plans (including 401(k) plans) are required to file an annual report with the Internal Revenue Service and the Department of Labor. There are certain exceptions and there are different schedules that must be filed, depending on the number of participants in the plan. We will review these details in this chapter.

Generally Form 5500 must be filed on or before the end of the seventh month after the end of the plan year (i.e., July 31 in the case of a calendar year plan). A postmark date from the U.S. postal service is used to determine whether or not the deadline has been satisfied (see penalties for late or missing filings below). Plans may obtain an automatic extension by filing Form 5558 with the IRS. Plans that have the same plan year as the plan sponsor's tax year will also be granted an automatic extension until the due date of the business tax return.

Form 5500 EZ

Form 5500 EZ is a short form that may be filed instead of Form 5500 if all of the following criteria are met:

- The plan is a one-participant plan

  The definition of a one-person plan for this purpose is:

  A plan that covers a single participant (and that participant's spouse) and that single participant (and/or spouse) is 100% owner of the business that sponsors the plan, *or*

A plan that covers one or more partners (and spouses) in a business partnership.

- The plan meets the minimum coverage requirements without being combined with any other plan that may be sponsored by the employer

- The plan does not provide benefits for anyone other than the one participant as defined above

- The plan does not cover a business that is a member of any of the following:

  - an affiliated service group

  - a controlled group

  - a group of business under common control

- The plan does not cover individuals of a business that uses leased employees

If a plan does not satisfy all five criteria stated above, Form 5500 EZ cannot be filed in lieu of Form 5500. If a plan is qualified to file Form 5500 EZ, there may be years where a filing is not required at all, as discussed below.

Exception for Years Where Plan Assets are Below $100,000

For plans that are eligible to file Form 5500EZ *and only those plans,* there is a complete exemption from having to file for a given year provided the following conditions are satisfied:

- The plan had total assets of $100,000 or less at the end of every plan year beginning on or after January 1, 1994

- The total of all "one-participant" plans sponsored by the same employer had a total of $100,000 or less at the end of every plan year beginning on or after January 1, 1994

- The plan does not have a funding deficiency for the plan year

- The plan year is not the *final* plan year, where all assets have been distributed.

Form 5500 and Applicable Schedules

Other than the exceptions noted above, Form 5500 must be filed each year. There are several references below to a "large plan" and a "small plan." For this purpose, generally a large plan is a plan with 100 or more participants at the beginning of the plan year and a small plan is a plan with less than 100 participants as of the beginning of the plan year.

There are two exceptions to this rule. The first is known as the 80-120 rule. If the number of participants is between 80 and 120 as of the beginning of the plan year, the plan may file the same form that was filed in the prior year. Therefore if the number of participants as of the beginning of the year is between 100 and 120 the plan may elect to file as a small plan, provided a small plan filing was prepared in the prior year. This election can continue for future filings, provided the number of participants does not exceed 120.

The second exception is applicable in the event of a short plan year (less than 7 months) for either the current or prior year. The plan may elect to defer the filing of the accountant's report; however, if such an election is made, the large plan filing must be made for the prior year regardless of how many participants there are at the beginning of the plan year.

In all cases, determining whether there is a large or small plan filing is unique to 401(k) plans. Individuals are counted as an "active participants" for this purpose if they are eligible to participate in the 401(k) plan. Therefore, in the case of a plan with 150 eligible participants, but only 20 participating, that plan would be subject to the large plan filing requirements.

Listed below are the Schedules that accompany Form 5500, and their purposes. For many Schedules there are differences depending on whether the plan is a "large plan" or a "small plan," the most notable being the requirement that accountant's opinion be attached to the return.

Schedule A (Insurance Information)

Schedule A must be completed for plans that contain insurance contracts for benefits and/or investments. A separate Schedule A must be filed for each carrier and different types of products also require separate Schedules. For example, if a plan has both life insurance policies and annuity contracts they must be reported on separate Schedule A's. As long as the contracts are in force, Schedule A must continue to be filed. This applies even to policies where there may be no further premium payments required.

Schedule A must be completed for both allocated and un-allocated contracts. Brokers and/or agents commissions are also reported on Schedule A. Recently there have been some concerns voiced by the DOL that all forms of compensation are not properly disclosed. The value of incentive fees paid over and above standard commissions must also be included in the disclosure.

Schedule B (Actuarial Certification Information)

Schedule B is not applicable to 401(k) plans. It is required to be filed plans subject to the minimum funding standard (IRC Section 412), including all defined benefit plans.

Schedule C (Service Provider Information)

Schedule C must be filed for plans with 100 or more participants. Small plans are not required to file Schedule C. Further, plans with 100 or more participants do not have to file Schedule C if:

> The plan has not paid directly or indirectly $5,000 or more to any service provider, *or*

> There has been no change in either the enrolled actuary or the accountant.

Schedule D (DFE/Participating Plan Information)

Schedule D must be filed by "Direct Filing Entities" and does not apply to single employer sponsored plans as a general rule. A filing must be made for each Master Trust Investment Account for which a regulated financial institution serves as a trustee or custodian and in which the assets of more than one plan sponsored by a single employer or group of employers under common control are held.

A regulated financial institution means a bank, trust company, or similar financial institution that is regulated, supervised and subject to periodic examination by a state or federal agency.

Some plans participate in certain trusts, accounts and other investment arrangements and may file a DFE Form 5500. These include:

- Common or Collective Trusts (CCT)

- Master Trust Investment Accounts (MTIA)

- Pooled Separate Accounts (PSA)

- 103-12 investment entities

If a CCT or PSA chooses not to file as a DFE, large employee plans (100 or more participants) must break out their percentage interest in the underlying asset of the CCT or PSA and report this on Schedule H.

Schedule G (Financial Transaction Schedule)

Large plans (100 or more participants) and DFE's are required to file Schedule G to report any of the following:

- Loans or fixed income obligations in default or classified as uncollectible

- Leases in default and/or uncollectible

- Non-exempt prohibited transactions

Participant loans that are secured by a portion of the participant's vested account balance are *not* required to be reported on Schedule G.

Schedule H (Financial Information—Large Plan)

All financial information regarding a plan is reported on Schedule H. This includes both a composition (Part I) and reconciliation (Part II) of plan assets from the beginning of the plan year to the end of the plan year.

Part III requires that an accountant's opinion be attached to the report. The accountant must indicate whether his or her opinion is a qualified or unqualified opinion. The Form 5500 will be deemed incomplete if an accountant's opinion is required and is not attached to the filing.

Part IV requires disclosure of certain transactions that may have occurred, as well as whether the plan is covered by a fidelity bond.

Schedule I (Financial Information –Small Plan)

All financial information for a small plan is required to be reported on Schedule I. This form is simpler than Schedule H (i.e. does not have a composition of assets section) and does *not* require that an accountant's opinion be attached.

Schedule P (Annual Return of Fiduciary of Employee Benefit Trust)

Plan fiduciaries and trustees of qualified plans must file a Schedule P. This Schedule requires that those handling the money for the plan disclose that they have provided the plan sponsor with sufficient information to prepare the return.

Filing the Schedule P also starts the clock running on the statute of limitations on any assessment and collection of tax that may be due under the trust.

Schedule R (Retirement Plan Information)

The Schedule R has to be filed for a 401(k) plan for a plan year in which distributions were paid. The employer identification number (EIN) on the Schedule R must be consistent with the EIN that was used on Form 1099-R to report the distributions.

If there were no distributions from the 401(k) plan for the plan year, a Schedule R does not have to be filed.

Schedule SSA (Identifying Participants with Deferred Vested Benefits)

Schedule SSA (SSA stands for Social Security Administration) identifies those individuals who are entitled to benefits from a plan and have not yet been paid. Generally a participant is included on Schedule SSA if he or she has not been paid the benefit by the filing due date (including extensions) following the plan year in which the participant had a separation of service.

Schedule SSA must be filed to:

- Report information about deferred vested participants

- Remove from the SSA records participants who were previously reported on Schedule SSA, but have since been paid

- Report any other information about previously reported participants.

Schedule T (Coverage Information)

The Schedule T asks for a demonstration that the plan satisfies the coverage requirements for the plan year. As noted throughout this book, the requirements of Section 410(b) of the Internal Revenue Code are a fundamental requirement for all qualified plans.

A plan that contains a 401(k) (elective deferral) provision, a 401(m) (matching contribution) provision and a 401(a) (profit sharing contribution) will be deemed three plans for purposes of the coverage rules. Each of these "component" plans will be required to demonstrate satisfaction of the coverage requirements on the Schedule T.

There are also certain defaults for purposes of Schedule T where the plan (or component plan) is deemed to satisfy the coverage requirements. The defaults are as follows:

- Plans with only highly compensated employees

- Plans where no highly compensated employee benefits during the plan year

- Plans that exclusively cover collectively bargained employees

- Plans that cover all of the non-highly compensated employees (other than those who do not meet the minimum age and service requirements defined by the plan)

- A plan that is satisfying the coverage requirements during a transition period due to an acquisition (as provided under Section 410(b)(6)(C) of the Internal Revenue Code).

Penalties for Noncompliance

Various penalties are imposed for not meeting the Form 5500 filing requirements (either late or nonfiling). One or more of the following penalties may be assessed or imposed:

- A penalty of up to $1,100 for each day a plan administrator fails or refuses to file a complete report (ERISA Sec. 502(c)(2))

- A penalty of $25 a day (up to a maximum of $15,000) (IRC Sec. 6652(e))

- A penalty of $1 per day (up to $5,000) for each participant who was not reported on Schedule SSA

- A penalty of $1,000 for not filing an actuarial statement (defined benefit plans only).

Any individual who willfully violates any provision of Part I, Title I of ERISA may be fined up to $100,000 or imprisoned up to 10 years, or both.

A penalty of up to $5,000, five years imprisonment, or both may be imposed for making any false statement or representation of fact, knowing it to be false or for knowingly concealing or not disclosing any fact required by ERISA.

Bedtime Reading Material

The "bible" or operations manual of a retirement plan is its trust document. This document comes in two basic varieties, prototype and custom document. The prototype is a "check the box" type approach, where the sponsoring entity (usually a financial institution) has had the options approved by the IRS. It is intended to be completed by a financial professional, but does not require the input of an attorney. A custom document will be tailored to the specific needs of the client and requires the involvement of either an attorney or actuary to complete and file the trust.

The simplest of the prototype plans are the standardized variety (see Appendix B). Every plan sponsor is entitled to use a standardized document once. After that, future prototypes must be of the non-standardized variety, requiring submission of changes and amendments to the IRS. Many self-employed plan sponsors attempt to complete their own prototype plan document. Given the intricacies of even the simplest 401(k) plan, this is fairly inadvisable. Should an employer have employees who are or may be eligible for participation, this is even more ill-advised.

Once the decision has been made to solicit the assistance of a professional, the most common document of choice becomes the volume submitter plan. This is a variation of the "check the box" approach where an attorney or actuary has the latitude to add and customize the structure. Through the modern miracle of word processing programs and merged documents, the end product is a document unique to the needs of that employer which may be used only by them.

Once of the largest advantages of this approach is that a power of attorney is typically filed in conjunction with the plan submission process. This allows the professional to represent the trustee in matters associated with the plan, including IRS matters. In addition, an attorney will request a federal tax identification number for the plan when filing the document and prepare the summary plan description (SPD).

Out with the Old, in the New

Having spent ten chapters of this book extolling the virtues of 401(k) plans, it occurs to us that a few lines should be spent on how to terminate or amend an existing plan to make room for a 401(k) plan. Should a firm have an existing defined benefit plan (DB) and want to completely replace it with a 401(k) (notwithstanding the details of Chapter 13), the only approach is to fully terminate the DB plan and start a new 401(k) plan.

For the sponsor of a money purchase plan (MPP), there are a few more options. Since an MPP is also a defined contribution plan, it may be restated into a profit sharing/401(k) plan. Reasons to do so would include a desire to *not* have employees vest fully as a result of the MPP being terminated, as well as the fact that a MPP may already offer a self directed investment feature.

Recall that an MPP requires that the sponsoring employer make a specific fixed annual deposit into the plan. The timing of when an allocation is deemed earned is specified in the plan trust document, and this date will affect the timing of when a plan can be amended from an MPP to a 401k. Of course the plan may be amended at any time, but if the employer wishes to avoid making the MPP allocation in the year of conversion, the plan will need to be amended before the MPP allocation accrues.

In a standardized prototype MPP, the deposit will automatically accrue for each participant following 500 hours of service during the plan year. A non-standardized prototype or individually drafted document can have either a last day of plan year provision (meaning that an employee must be employed on the last day of a plan year to receive an allocation of a company deposit) or require 1,000 hours of participation before accruing a benefit.[1] For most plans without a last day of plan year provision, this effectively means that any plan amendment adding a 401(k) feature must be adopted no later than six months into the plan year to convert from an MPP.

Of course, profit sharing plans (PSPs) are the easiest type of plan to include a 401(k) provision. First of all, all 401(k) plans are, by definition, a subset of PSPs. In addition, the document issues are of less concern, as they have no stated requirement that a company deposit be made in any given year. So, adding a 401(k) feature is a snap for a PSP.

In all instances, written notice must be provided to plan participants no later than 15 days prior to the accrual of an obligation to make a deposit for that year.

Tax Credits for New Plans

How cool is this—the IRS even helps to subsidize the establishment of a new plan by a firm that has never had one.[2] Employers with fewer than 100 employees who have never sponsored a retirement program before, may receive a tax credit of up to $500 per year for the first three years of their plan. The intention is to create an incentive to establishing a plan by providing a tax credit for start-up costs. Bear in mind that a tax credit is different than a deduction and, in exchange for the tax credit, an employer cannot also deduct those start-up fees for which the tax credit is being taken.

This provision applies to SIMPLE IRAs and simplified employee pensions (SEPs) as well as 403(b) and qualified plans. Other provisions of this law[3] also provide small employers with relief from IRS user fees for determination letter filings for new plans.

Chapter Endnotes

1. ERISA Section 204(h).
2. See IRC Sec. 45E.
3. The Economic Growth and Tax Relief Reconciliation Act of 2001.

Chapter 12

Acquisitions, Dispositions and Owners

As we all have undoubtedly experienced, rarely do things go strictly as planned. In our experience, this is typically the case for most retirement plans. Notwithstanding the fact that one of us is an actuary, trained in the fine art of "reasonable guessing" and probabilities versus certainties, we have learned to be flexible. Thus, this chapter was born. Aside from the obvious—companies change form, structure, ownership, and markets—profitability can change (up, down, sideways, out) and people change (new management in, old management out, old management back in, etc). Responding to and planning for that change is, in itself, an art form. This chapter describes some of our experience dealing with changes.

Plan Mergers

If a business purchases another business, and either one or both of those businesses sponsor a 401(k) plan, certain steps need to be taken to insure compliance. Under the coverage requirements (IRC Section 410(b)) there is a 1-year transition rule that allows the new entity to assume its new identity as a plan sponsor. The transition period extends to the last day of the plan year following the year of acquisition. For example for a calendar year plan in which an acquisition took place on February 1, 2005, the transition period would apply through December 31, 2006. Therefore, the new sponsor would first be required to satisfy the coverage rules under the new combined business structure for the 2007 plan year. Under this example, the 401(k) discrimination test, the match discrimination test and all the availability tests would have to be satisfied on an employer wide basis for the 2007 plan year. (See Chapters 4, 5 and 6 for details on discrimination testing.)

Same Desk Rule

Prior to the Economic Growth and Tax Relief Reconciliation Act of 2001 (EGTRRA), there was some confusion about an employee's ability to receive a distribution from a 401(k) plan where there was a change in the plan sponsor (due to a merger). The triggering event that caused confusion was the definition of an employee's "separation from service." For example, if Company B acquired Company A and Employee X did the same job that he or she always did, but now had a new Employer, was there a separation from service? The answer is that there was a separation of service of Employee X if you look only at his tenure with Company A. This phenomenon was known as the "same desk rule" and it was not the intent of Congress under such circumstances to trigger a distributable event. EGTRRA changed the language from "separation from service" to "severance of employment" which clarifies that an employee must actually sever employment (regardless of who is the employer sponsoring the plan) in order to qualify as a distributable event.

Plans can be merged under the new sponsor, provided the account balances after the merger are the same as the account balances before the merger for all participants. If all monies are fully vested, there is no filing necessary to report the merger. However if there are monies that are not 100% nonforfeitable, Form 5310 must be filed to report the merger. The merger will also be reflected on Form 5500 for both receiving plan and the plan that will cease to exist.

Different Types of Plan Sponsors

The plan sponsor can be any type of business entity. This includes corporations (either S or C), partnerships, sole proprietors, limited liability companies (LLCs) and limited liability partnerships (LLPs). In addition, nonprofit entities can now sponsor 401(k) plans as can unions. There is virtually no restriction as to the type of private entity that can sponsor a 401(k) plan.

In all cases, in order for compensation to be eligible for a qualified plan, it must be earned income subject to Social Security tax withholding. Therefore, passive income, dividend income (including income reported to shareholders of an S corporation not reported on a W-2) and any other remuneration that is not subject to Social Security tax withholding cannot be used as compensation for any qualified plan. In addition, 401(k) contributions, while deductible to the employer for federal income tax purposes (as well as most state and local income taxes), are not deductible for purposes of computing the Social Security tax. The following example will illustrate this point.

> *Example 1:* John Doe is an employee for AB Co. and has a gross W-2 of $50,000. John has made contributions of $4,000 during the year. There is no other income or deductions applicable to John. His W-2 will reflect $46,000 in Box 1 (amount subject to federal income tax) and $50,000 in Box 5 (amount subject to Social Security tax).

Self-employed individuals must adhere to a unique set of rules in order to determine the amount that is eligible for a qualified plan contribution. For this purpose self-employed individuals are those whose earned income is reported on Schedule C, as well as partners in a partnership and members of LLCs and LLPs. The income tax deduction for self-employed individuals is taken on the individual tax return, not on the business tax return.

This type of reporting is in contrast to that of an owner of a corporation, for whom the deduction for a qualified plan contribution is taken on the business tax return and is not reflected on the individual tax return. For example if a one-person corporation has $100,000 of profit after all expenses (besides salary, pension and payroll taxes) and the business owner wants to make a contribution to a qualified plan, that $100,000 will be divided between salary, qualified plan contribution and payroll taxes. In a corporation, one-half of the Social Security tax is paid by the corporation and is a deductible expense. In addition, the 401(k) contribution reduces the W-2 for income tax purposes, as stated above.

In an effort to create "parity" for qualified plans between the unincorporated business and incorporated business, the qualified plan deduction for the self-employed individual must reduce the net earned income from self-employment for qualified plan purposes. The following example illustrates the calculation of a maximum contribution for a one-person 401(k) plan that includes a profit sharing contribution.

> *Example 2:* Dr. Wilson is self-employed, 30 years old and has no employees. Her net earned income from self-employment for 2005 is

$147,555.88. Dr. Wilson will be able to make a maximum contribution of $42,000 with this income as follows:

Net Schedule C:	$147,555.88
½ FICA Tax:	$ 7,555.88
Net Income after ½ FICA tax:	$140,000.00
401(k) Contribution:	$ 14,000.00
Profit Sharing Contribution:	$ 28,000.00
Net Income after Profit Sharing:	$112,000.00

Note the 25% maximum for the profit sharing contribution is satisfied due to the fact that $28,000 when divided by $112,000 yields 25%. In addition as described in Chapter 2, the 401(k) contribution of $14,000 does not impact the calculation of the 25% maximum deduction limit.

Controlled Groups, Affiliated Service Groups and Family Attribution

An employer must cover a required number of nonhighly compensated employees. The exact number of non-highly compensated employees that have to benefit under a qualified plan is a function of the number of highly compensated employees that benefit during each plan year.

Two or more business entities (incorporated or unincorporated) must be combined and treated as a single employer if they constitute a controlled group or an affiliated service group.

Essentially, two or more entities are a controlled group if they are owned by the same or very similar individuals or entities. A parent-controlled group is defined as one business owning 80% or more of another business. A brother-sister controlled group occurs when the same five or fewer individuals own 80% or more of two (or more) entities.

In the determination of ownership, the family attribution rules apply. Ownership by spouses, lineal ascendants and descendants (under the age of 21), parents and grandparents of 5% owners is aggregated for this purpose. Ownership by trusts for the benefit of children or grandchildren are also included for this purpose. These rules are in place to ward off employers who are seeking to avoid providing benefits to employees (or certain employees) by establishing a separate business.

A married couple with two separate businesses, in general will not constitute a controlled group. However, if that married couple have a minor child, the rules require attribution of each of the parent's ownership to the child (or children). In effect, the child owns both businesses and therefore (as odd as it may seem) there is an unexpected controlled group.

Under this scenario any qualified plan sponsored by either (or both) entities would have to be treated as though there was a single employer (coverage, discrimination tests etc., would have to be applied by combining the two business entities). In today's world of second marriages, this is often a compliance challenge. Few are aware of these regulations, and often fail to adjust their plans to place both plans into compliance.

The affiliated service group rules are not as clear and finite as the controlled group rules. Very often the determination of whether or not two entities constitute an affiliated service group requires a legal opinion. The existence of an affiliated service group between two or more businesses depends upon the working relationship between the entities, whether or not they share business locations, employees, clients and management services.

Once again these rules are in place to prevent employers from creating a business entity that can sponsor a plan, in an effort to provide less or no benefits to rank and file employees.

Chapter 13

Hooking It Up With the Big Daddy — 401(k) and Defined Benefit

As mentioned in Chapter 2, the deduction limits for 401(k) plans were dramatically liberalized under the Economic Growth and Tax Reconciliation Relief Act of 2001 (EGTRRA). The elective deferrals are no longer considered an "employer" deduction for purposes of the single plan limit or the multi-plan limit. In addition, the combined plan (defined benefit and defined contribution) limit for an individual under Section 415(e) was completely repealed as part of the Taxpayer Relief Act of 1997, effective for years beginning after 1999. The road has been paved for combining 401(k) plans and defined benefit plans to produce some exciting results. Several different plan design options are discussed in this chapter.

Why a Defined Benefit Plan?

A defined benefit (DB) plan introduces a few key elements into the formula. The first is security. DB plans provide a fixed benefit to all participants payable at a specific point in the future. The investment risk (and potential investment gain) is borne by the plan. If an actuary assumes 6% growth on assets, and the plan earns 5%, the employer must deposit enough to fund the shortfall. Conversely, if the plan earns 7%, future deposits will be reduced by these investment gains.

Benefits provided under a defined benefit may not be reduced. With an increasing amount of service with the employer and participation in the plan, a participant's benefit is accrued or earned. DB plans have very strict guidelines under which accrued benefits may not be reduced. This provision has often been one of the barriers to a DB plan as those defined as highly compensated employees may receive their benefit only after others have been paid out or adequately funded.

The major consideration to sponsoring a DB plan is the fact that it tends to favor not only more highly compensated employees, but also those closer to retirement. If the longer term, and typically older employees are the target group to favor, a DB does the trick. This is due to the fact that the closer one is to retirement, the greater the deposit that will be due on their behalf. More often than not, sponsors of DBs will be firms with consistent and steady cash flow to help weather the higher funding requirements.

As was mentioned at the start of this book, defined benefit plans were the primary type of retirement program two decades ago. Given the desire for security and the loosening of the combined plan rules, many employers are gravitating back towards a DB as either their primary plan, or one linked with a defined contribution (DC) plan.

Defined Benefit and 401(k): All Eligible Employees Covered Under Both Plans

As noted earlier, the deduction limit in this case is not impacted by the 401(k) plan at all, provided there is no employer contribution to the 401(k) plan. The deduction limit for a defined benefit plan is the same as if the defined benefit plan stood on its own. Therefore there is no specific percentage of payroll deduction limitation in this case. On the other hand if there is an employer contribution made (or accrued) to the 401(k) plan, there is a limit on the deducible amount. That limit is the greater of 25% of eligible compensation or the amount necessary to meet the minimum funding requirements of the defined benefit plan. The examples below illustrate these points.

Example 1: Company LMN sponsors both a defined benefit and a 401(k) plan for the 2005 tax year. Assume that both the company and the plan are operating on a calendar year. The eligible payroll is $2,000,000 and the 401(k) elective deferrals are $250,000. In addition, the actuary for the defined benefit plan has determined the range of contributions for the 2005 plan year is $700,000-$800,000. Company LMN contributes $750,000 to the defined benefit plan prior to the due date of the tax return, including extensions. Since there is no employer contribution being made to the 401(k) plan for 2005, the 401(k) plan has no impact on the tax deduction of $750,000 that Company LMN takes on its 2005 tax return.

Example 2: Assume the same facts as Example 1, except that the Company LMN 401(k) plan has a matching contribution of 50 cents for every $1 of elective deferral contributions. The matching contribution is $125,000 and it is paid throughout the course of the 2005 plan year. Since the $125,000 match was paid in 2005, the company has every intention of deducting that expense for the 2005 tax year.

The minimum required contribution is $700,000 and must be paid no later than September 15, 2006. Since $700,000 is the maximum tax deductible limit for 2005 (i.e. the greater of 25% of payroll or the amount necessary to meet the minimum funding requirement under the defined benefit plan) and the $125,000 matching contribution must be applied against the $700,000 limit, Company LMN pays $575,000 prior to March 15, 2006 (the due date of the company's tax return) and pays the $125,000 required to complete its funding obligation prior to September 15, 2006. The $125,000 that is paid after March 15, 2006 and prior to September 15, 2006 will be deducted on the company's 2006 tax return.

Example 3: Assume the same facts as Example 2, except that the acceptable range of contributions for the defined benefit plan is $300,000-400,000. In this case the Company deduction limit is $500,000 (i.e. 25% of eligible payroll) and the Company can contribute $375,000 to the defined benefit plan, prior to the due date of the tax return (including extensions) and deduct the full amount.

Floor/Offset Plan

A floor offset plan is a combination of a defined benefit and defined contribution plan where the benefits derived from the defined benefit plan are "offset" by the converted account balances from a defined contribution plan. In order for a floor offset plan to be granted safe harbor treatment under the non-discrimination rules all participants have to be covered by both plans and the same set of assumptions have to be used for funding the benefits and converting the account balances to benefits for offset purposes. In addition, 401(k) elective deferral contributions and matching contributions *cannot* be used to offset benefits that would otherwise be payable from the defined benefit plan. Therefore, in order to make use of the floor offset plan a profit sharing contribution (which can include the 3% safe harbor contribution—see Chapter 5) would have to be part of the plan. The mechanics of this type of plan can be illustrated by the following example. In a safe harbor floor offset plan, the two-plan deduction rule applies as described above.

Example 4: Listed below is the census data for Company RST.

Step 1: To compute the profit sharing contribution, project that contribution to retirement age by converting the projected account balance into a pension benefit:

Name	Retirement Age	Age	Salary	Profit Sharing Contribution	Projected Account	Converted Account
EE#1	55	65	$210,000	$21,000	$264,136	$26,414
EE#2	40	65	$150,000	$15,000	$715,906	$71,591
EE#3	40	65	$75,000	$7,500	$357,953	$35,795
EE#4	35	65	$60,000	$6,000	$398,633	$39,863
EE#5	30	65	$50,000	$5,000	$451,601	$45,160
EE#6	25	65	$35,000	$3,500	$422,799	$42,280
Total:			$580,000	$58,000		

Step 2: Compute the defined benefit plan formula before and after the offset from the profit sharing plan as indicated below. The benefit formula before the offset is 45% of salary.

Name	Retirement Age	Age	Salary	Converted Account	Defined Benefit Before Offset	Defined Benefit After Offset
EE#1	55	65	$210,000	$26,414	$94,500	$68,359
EE#2	40	65	$150,000	$71,591	$67,500	$0
EE#3	40	65	$75,000	$35,795	$33,750	$0
EE#4	35	65	$60,000	$39,863	$27,000	$0
EE#5	30	65	$50,000	$45,160	$22,500	$0
EE#6	25	65	$35,000	$42,280	$15,750	$0
Total:			$580,000			

Step 3: Compute the cost for the defined benefit plan based upon the fact that the sole participant who is not completely offset by the converted account of the profit sharing plan is Employee #1.

Name	Salary	Defined Benefit After Offset	Level Deposit Defined	Profit Sharing Contribution Benefit	Total
EE#1	$210,000	$68,359	$54,349	$21,000	$75,349
EE#2	150,000	0	0	15,000	15,000
EE#3	75,000	0	0	7,500	7,500
EE#4	60,000	0	0	6,000	6,000
EE#5	50,000	0	0	5,000	5,000
EE#6	35,000	0	0	3,500	3,500
Total:	$580,000		$54,349	$58,000	$112,349

For purposes of this example, it was assumed that the rate of return for projecting the profit sharing account balance and funding the defined benefit plan was 5%.

Defined Benefit and 401(k): Not All Employees Covered Under Both Plans

All qualified plans are subject to minimum coverage requirements explained in Chapter 6. Defined benefit plans are subject to an additional requirement: every defined benefit plan must cover at least 40% of the otherwise eligible employees (or, if less, 50 employees—see IRC Sec. 401(a)(26)). It is possible to create a situation where some of the employees of a company are covered by one plan and others are covered by another plan. In addition to the bright line numerical tests defined in the Internal Revenue Code for minimum coverage, there are other factors that need to be considered if the group of employees is going to be divided into multiple plans. Factors such as age discrimination, sex discrimination and other considerations need to be reviewed with the clients and their counsel if appropriate.

Since 401(k) and 401(m) contributions are deemed separate plans under the coverage rules, it is possible to allow all employees to be part of a 401(k) plan with a matching contribution, while excluding a non-discriminatory class (or classes) of employees from receiving a profit sharing contribution. These excluded employees can be part of a defined benefit plan that excludes those covered by the profit sharing plan. If there is no "overlap" in coverage between participants of the defined benefit plan and those receiving an employer contribution in the defined contribution plan, the deduction limit for multiple plans *does not apply*.

Therefore, if there are no participants who are both earning a benefit in the defined benefit plan and receiving an employer contribution in the 401(k) plan, the deduction limit for the defined benefit is computed without regard to the 401(k) plan and the deduction limit for the 401(k) plan is computed without regard to the defined benefit plan.

Understanding the manner in which these two distinctly different plans operate can be a powerful advantage for the advisor looking to assist a profitable client in building a truly meaningful benefit program.

Chapter 14

Size Matters

In a world where technology and the law of the microchip keep driving things smaller, it is logical that the same has happened to the world of retirement plans. Arguably, it all began with the Self-Employed Individuals Tax Retirement Act of 1962. This act, first introduced as HR-10, created the retirement plans of the same name, also known as Keogh plans. This brought some degree of parity between the plans available to self-employed individuals and those available to employees. Prior to the 1962 Act, unincorporated and small businesses did not have the same range of retirement plan options available to them as larger corporations.

Keogh plans initially operated under a simplified version of the post-ERISA rules that governed larger corporate plans. Then, with passage of the Economic Recovery Tax Act of 1981 (ERTA) and the Tax Equity and Fiscal Responsibility Act of 1982 (TEFRA), large and small plans were brought into much greater parity. Essentially, what was available for large plans became available for small ones. At this stage the planning tool then known as a Keogh plan became somewhat obsolete.

Hal's Corner Deli could now offer the same retirement plan as IBM. Understandably, it took several years for this concept to catch on. Even today, many refer to Keogh plans as the generic term for retirement plans of self-employed individuals. Predictably, it began with money purchase and profit sharing plans (this was in an age when the two were combined to maximize the deductible limits and plan flexibility). Soon, one and two-person defined benefit plans came into vogue.

Fast forward to the modern world of 401(k) plans. As already detailed, company sponsored and funded plans have become the exception rather than the rule. In a fee-sensitive world, a full blown 401(k) proved to be too costly for many smaller firms.

Solo 401(k) Plan

Enter the "Uni-K" or Solo 401(k) plan. Essentially this type of plan provides for a one-person 401(k) plan. Many think that these plans were given their life under the Economic Growth and Tax Reconciliation Relief Act of 2001 (EGTRRA). The truth is that there has never been a statutory minimum to the number of employees that are required for a 401(k) plan. In fact, prior to EGTRRA, we had several one and two person 401(k) plans for the flexibility provided by 401(k) plans.

Prior to the passage of EGTRRA in 2001, the annual additions limit for defined contribution plans (and therefore 401(k) plans) was the lesser of 25% of pay or $35,000. As detailed in Chapter 2, EGTRRA removed the 25% limit on the percentage of pay that may be deferred into a 401(k). Thus, with the statutory limit of $14,000 for 2005, a self-employed individual earning $28,000 could defer 50% of it into a 401(k). In the hands of the marketing geniuses at major financial institutions, this became a uni-k or solo-k.

An example may be the best way to understand the powerful opportunity this presents. Fred is an employee of a large corporation that does not have a 401(k) plan. Recently he began a side business from his basement that makes him about $25,000 per year of net Schedule C income (after his ordinary business expenses). By adopting a 401(k) plan (which some may call a uni-k plan); he can defer $14,000 per year. This would reduce his taxable income by more than 50%.

This is before Fred contemplates adding a profit sharing option, for an additional 20%. Prior to doing that he may want to take advantage of the $4,000 catch-up contribution (in 2005) he is entitled to make after he has reached age 50. The bottom line is that the uni-k can allow him to defer most of his taxable income, with little or no administrative cost.

What A Lovely Couple

Joy comes from sharing, and the true power of the uni-k comes from a scenario where a spouse can be included on the payroll, even for a de minimis amount, which can be deferred into a 401(k) plan. Assume that after about three years in business, Fred's business has grown and needs some help, so his wife, Wilma, begins to help keep the books. They agree on the princely sum of $1,300 per month or $15,600 per year.

As fate has it, Wilma can defer virtually all of her income into Fred's plan. A word of caution—Fred would be mistaken to simply pay his beloved $14,000 per year so that she could defer all of it into the uni-k plan. When calculating the required payroll associated with her employment and desire to defer $14,000 annually, Fred must be certain to account for her payroll taxes. Assume that it is only FICA at 7.65%. At her salary rate of $15,600 per year, the taxes would be $1,194. This will leave her $14,406 of income, the lion's share of which could be deferred into the uni-k.

Between Fred and Wilma, over two-thirds of their combined income has been deferred from current taxation. Thus, the potential range of plans available to the small business owner is a far cry from the initial concept of parity.

Smaller Firms

Many of the concepts contained in this book (safe harbor plans, new comparability, floor offset with a defined benefit plan, etc.) fit best with the small sized form (under 100 employees), where typically the business owner and decision maker are one and the same. This group often looks at a retirement plan as an employee benefit program as well as a tax advantaged savings vehicle.

Much of what we have discussed has been geared towards this group and, from our perspective, this market is the area where there is some significant room for growth. Fewer small companies have already started 401(k) plans than mid to larger size companies. In addition, our experience has demonstrated that many smaller firms who are already sponsoring a 401(k) plan are very dissatisfied with their program. Neither the investment product, the administration, nor the plan communication (sometimes none of the three) get passing grades.

This creates a significant amount of opportunity for the advisor looking to work within this segment of the market. The common denominator among many plan sponsors with whom we have worked has been a lack of understanding of what they have. For them, there is often little value derived from the fees and time that they invest into sponsoring the plan. Unfortunately, in an age where the difference between right and privilege is often confused, these plan sponsors rarely can completely get rid of their programs, and are often forced into trolling the market for a better set of options.

Mid-Size Companies

Like the forgotten middle child, the mid-sized company (100 to 2,500 employees) is in a unique position when it comes to retirement plans. They are often too big to take advantage of many of the design techniques that we have reviewed in this book, and they are too small to gain entry to the low-fee, minimal cost programs that are available to their larger brethren.

The fact is that a matching deposit or safe harbor profit sharing approach can cost a larger firm huge amounts on an annual basis. In addition, these firms tend to have the most difficulties passing their actual deferral percentage test (ADP—see Chapter 4) in an accommodating way for the highly compensated employees (HCEs). Take into account that the threshold compensation level for HCEs in 2005 is $95,000 of income in the prior plan year, and the fact that in some larger metropolitan areas this is barely a large enough salary to squeak by, and you realize that many of these firms have a challenge even allowing their key folks to fully participate in the plan.

For this group, we have found that the safe harbor matching formula (dollar for dollar on the first 3% of pay deferred and 50 cents per dollar on the next 2% deferred) is a great solution. Assuming that a traditional match fails to do the trick, the safe harbor match will remove the firm from the constraints of the ADP test, and allow all HCEs to defer as much as they wish (subject, of course, to the current annual threshold). For these firms, the safe harbor has been a true saving grace. Often, the emphasis on sophisticated profit sharing formulae is not as significant, and there is even further dependence on the communication and enrollment skills discussed in Chapter 10.

The mid size company that sponsors a 401(k) plan must always be demonstrating that the plan has relevance and that the costs associated with such a plan justify its existence. Here, administrative costs are often boiled down to a per head amount, and plan efficiency is dependent upon acceptance by the rank and file. Of course, you are also appealing to a more broadly defined universe of employees in what we define as a mid-sized firm. Nonetheless, many find organizations of this size a true sweet spot. The overall plan asset base tends to be fairly significant and, of course, the cross marketer has many opportunities available to engage in ancillary consulting or product sales to the diverse group of employees.

Big Firms

Pity the poor giant in a land of the normal sized. So many larger firms today offer sophisticated and technologically advanced 401(k) programs. These larger firms (2,500 and more employees) seem to have the world at their fingertips. Many receive the most favorable institutional pricing from their asset managers. Often "free" recordkeeping and plan administration is thrown into the deal.

Online services are state of the art, including online enrollment, electronic account access integrated with the firm's web site, and daily downloads to financial monitoring tools such as Quicken or Microsoft Money. Asset allocation and portfolio design tools are often provided from third party vendors such as m-Power or Morningstar. All these bells and whistles and fancy goodies, what problems could they have?

Well surprise of all surprises, many studies (and our first-hand experience) tell us that participants of plans sponsored by large firms are often among the most confused and ill-advised. Often, participants in these plans feel neglected and uncertain that the choices they have made are truly in their interest.

More and more Fortune 500 firms are now offering concierge-like planning services centered around a personalized and in-person planning process designed to integrate one's benefit work with personal planning. Traditionally included as part of an executive perk package for higher-end employees, these services are also being included in many flex-benefit menus (often for an additional fee).

Nonetheless, if the past continues to be a prelude to the future, the large plan participant will receive access to the services that they desire. In addition, these enhancements will eventually trickle their way down through to the medium and small plan markets.

Chapter 15

Moving from Suspect, to Prospect, to Client

The ideal corporate prospect for a 401(k) plan falls into one of two camps: those who have a retirement plan and those who don't. Basically, one of the beauties of the retirement plan marketplace is that every corporation is a valid prospect. Many small business owners have yet to establish a plan, either because they consider themselves too small or perhaps they fail to understand just how reasonably one could be established. Many firms without plans are also under the misconception that the sponsoring employer must match the deferrals of the employees. Although doing so often helps to increase participation, it is by no means required.

There is a tremendous amount of misconception within the business community regarding details associated with qualified retirement plans. Not just limited to 401(k) plans, many firms currently provide staff with access to a retirement program that is underutilized. Often, these include features such as self-directed investments, in-service distributions and portability, which are not adequately emphasized by current plan administrators One of our common comments to prospects is that we help to put the employee back into the employee benefit plan.

In our practice, about 60% of the new engagements begun each year are actually deemed takeover plans, in the sense that they already offer some type of retirement program. Often the ownership or management group share a common concern that the fees they spend administering their programs are poor investments, given either the low plan participation rates or inability to allocate

FIGURE 15.1

Associated Benefit Consultants

Pensions and Employee Benefits

Client Name	Contact
Phone	Street Address
Fax	City
Email	State

Last Name	First Name	Date of Birth	Date of Hire	Current Salary	Prior Year Salary	Projected Deferrals

Associated Benefit Consultants
White Plains, NY

corporate contributions in line with management objectives. More on the latter below, but the former is readily addressable by the benefits consultant who—after listening to employee concerns and objectives—is willing to take a proactive stance.

Collecting Data

After identifying the perfect candidate for a new or takeover 401(k) plan, the next challenge becomes knowing what to say and how to say it. For our purposes, we will keep the universe divided into the two camps already mentioned, and detail what is needed to properly prepare a plan for each. "Should we really sponsor a retirement plan?" Often many of our relationships begin with this basic question. Those who have yet to sponsor a 401(k) plan probably consider that they are improperly sized to adopt one.

As such, it all begins with a census request. These come in many shapes, sizes and formats, but the necessary basic data is pretty similar for all of them. Specifically, data must be gathered around the following areas: who is on payroll, when were they born, how long have they been there, and how much are they paid?

A sample census request is shown in Figure 15.1. Other than the most basic data, additional useful information includes prior years' compensation and any ownership interest in the firm. Prior year compensation is used specifically to determine who is classified as a highly compensated employee. Of course, ownership is an indicator not only for purposes of defining control and status as a key employee, but it also may serve as an indicator of who should be favored if any type of advanced profit sharing allocation is created.

Finally, in the event that the potential plan is a 401(k), some type of estimate of projected deferrals is helpful as well. Whenever possible, this is an important question to ask employees in advance of holding a full-blown enrollment meeting. Often we will provide the trustee with a simple one page informal questionnaire to be completed by employees.

Constructed in a "soft" manner, the goal is to gauge the potential popularity of a 401(k) plan among employees. Would they be interested in the firm sponsoring a 401(k) plan? If they could participate, what is an approximate percentage of pay that they would possibly defer? We try to be clear that this is a preliminary survey and should a plan be offered, a more formal enrollment process will be held. In addition, although there is no promise being made by the employer to offer a match, we often gauge how critical it is that the firm makes a deposit in order for the employee to participate.

Processing the Data

Now that you have it – what do you do with the data? In simplest terms – get thee to an actuary. It is critical that someone or some firm that is expert in these areas design the plan. Many of the advanced planning techniques detailed in the earlier chapters of this book will help to distinguish you from the "vendors" who have entered the 401(k) market solely to gather more assets. This distinction will help you be perceived as a true "401(k) Advisor."

Instructions for the plan design specialist should include what the overall objectives are of the plan. Will it function solely as an employee benefit program, or is there a desire to reward certain key employees? Who, if anyone, should be favored? When it comes to the company deposit, what is the overall budget? Is this a firm commitment, or is the preference to wait and see what profits are like on an annual basis? Are they comfortable with a minimal deposit of 3% of pay? Chapter 5 explains the magic of a 3% contribution.

Concurrent with this effort, details such as plan investment options, trust design considerations, and administrative details should all be considered. These are also detailed throughout the chapters of this book.

Show Me What You Have

Once the data has been compiled and the plan properly designed, we provide a quite simple summary for the employer, explaining all of their options and a basic fee quote. An example of this summary is shown in Figure 15.2. Typically, we are comparing one or two options to a basic 401(k) profit sharing combination.

When detailing the plan, we attempt to relate the fact that the simplest approach is to keep all pay expressed as a percentage of compensation. In addition, we prefer to express each person's allocation as related to the overall corporate plan deposit. (i.e., as a percentage of the total). This is significant when designing a plan with the objective of a greater allocation to key people. Tools that allow us to maximize this design include new comparability or age based profit sharing designs and, of course, safe harbor 401(k) features (see Chapters 4 and 5).

A quick word on such plan redesigns: the beauty of a profit sharing plan is that often we can maintain the same budget and increase the allocation to key people *or* increase the overall budget, while also increasing the allocation to key staff and/or owners. Flexibility, both in terms of the amount deposited, as well as the intended allocation, is one of the main advantages that we introduce to our clients.

FIGURE 15.2

My Best Case

RETIREMENT PLAN OPTIONS

		401(k) w/PROFIT SHARING				SAFE HARBOR 401(k) w/ ADVANCED PSP				
EMPLOYEE	2005 PROJ COMP	401(k) DEFERRAL	PSP DEPOSIT	TOTAL	% OF TOT	401(k) DEFERRAL	SAFE HARBOR	PSP DEPOSIT	TOTAL	% OF TOT
Owner A	210,000	14,000	28,000	42,000	17%	14,000	6,300	21,850	42,150	30%
Owner B	210,000	14,000	28,000	42,000	17%	14,000	6,300	21,850	42,150	30%
EE A	29,191	3,795	3,795	3,795	2%	N/A	876	420	1,296	1%
EE B	51,124	2,400	6,646	6,646	3%	N/A	1,534	736	2,270	2%
EE C	113,414	8,624	14,744	14,744	6%	N/A	3,402	1,633	5,036	4%
EE D	76,766	4,350	9,980	9,980	4%	N/A	2,303	1,105	3,408	2%
EE E	21,000		2,730	2,730	1%	N/A	630	302	932	1%
EE F	108,414	4,120	14,094	14,094	6%	N/A	3,252	1,561	4,814	3%
EE G	164,414	6,360	21,374	21,374	9%	N/A	4,932	2,368	7,300	5%
EE H	73,366	1,850	9,538	9,538	4%	N/A	2,201	1,056	3,257	2%
EE I	70,542	8,400	9,170	9,170	4%	N/A	2,116	1,016	3,132	2%
EE J	200,000	14,000	26,000	26,000	10%	N/A	6,000	1,850	7,850	6%
EE K	39,832	1,950	5,178	5,178	2%	N/A	1,195	574	1,769	1%
EE L	30,749		3,997	3,997	2%		922	443	1,365	1%
EE M	32,373	3,000	4,208	4,208	2%		971	466	1,437	1%
EE N	20,166		2,622	2,622	1%		605	290	895	1%
EE O	13,077		1,700	1,700	1%		392	188	581	0%
EE P	20,749		2,697	2,697	1%		622	299	921	1%
EE Q	75,949	4,500	9,873	9,873	4%		2,278	1,094	3,372	2%
EE R	50,542	5,000	6,570	6,570	3%		1,516	728	2,244	2%
EE S	72,000		9,360	9,360	4%		2,160	1,037	3,197	2%
TOTAL				$248,277			$50,510	$60,867	$139,377	

Fee Structure

Again, in the interests of keeping it simple, we offer a very basic fee structure. All of the plans we administer are billed a flat dollar amount for the plan, followed by a per person charge. There is an installation fee, typically charged for setting up the plan on the database, as well as for the books and administrative files.

The widest range of fees is typically determined by the type of trust document that is selected. The range of options spans from standardized prototype provided by a product vendor to a custom designed document. For a sample plan document, see Appendix B. As an aside, we do not include the IRS submission fees in our formal fee quote, but mention the fact that certain choices may involve an additional fee.

A brief word on creating the legal document: this may well be the most important, but often mishandled, step of establishing a plan. Often the trust document does not square with the intended design or current administrative practices. Establishing the provisions of the plan is not as simple as many "check the box" prototypes have led people to believe. Figure 15.3 shows a sample of the specification request that we typically provide to our ERISA attorneys.

Figure 15.4 shows a sample of a fee quote. As this quote indicates, we offer full service administration. The client's responsibility is to simply fund the plan, report the census data to us annually, and verify that no funds have been deposited outside of the specified plan investment vehicle(s) (assuming that we are involved with the investment process). In return, all forms such as 5500s are provided on a signature-ready basis, requiring no client input or editing.

Harnessing the Takeover Plan

In the majority of circumstances, our new relationships tend to be clients who already have a plan in place. The most common source of their discontent is either a lack of understanding of the plan by employees, or a lack of appreciation. Ultimately, this leads to a lack of participation, which manifests itself in the inability of key people or highly compensated employees to fully participate.

Working with the takeover plan often involves a thorough analysis of plan design details, as well as the all-important and powerful profit sharing allocation. Typically, there is a need to beef up the plan communication process. As men-

---

FIGURE 15.3

401(k) Specifications

▶ EFFECTIVE DATE: January 1, 2005

▶ ELIGIBILITY: Current EE's – Immediate
New Hire's After 1 Year Service

▶ ENTRY DATES: Jan1   July 1

▶ COMPENSATION DEFINITION: Total W2

▶ VESTING: Graded 6 yr based on service

▶ LOAN PROVISION: Yes with minimum acct balance of 10k

▶ HARDSHIP WITHDRAWAL PROVISION: Yes

▶ ROLLOVER PROVISION: Yes

▶ VALUATION FREQUENCY: Annual

▶ TYPE OF INVESTMENT CONTRACT(S):   XYZ Investments, inc.

▶ CAN PARTICIPANTS DIRECT ACCOUNTS? Yes

▶ PRIOR PLAN?   NO

▶ MATCHING CONTRIBUTION: Safe Harbor/Discretionary

▶ ALLOCATION OF PSP CONTRIBUTION: New Comparability – 3 groups

▶ TRUSTEES: Jim Smith/Kelly Jones

---

tioned, there is an art to putting the employee back into your employee benefit plan. Of course, getting your arms around a plan that has been in existence is considerably more complicated than starting with a nice blank slate, as in a new plan.

To that end, we utilize a checklist (see Figure 15.5) of information that, should be provided in addition to the basic census data. Although fairly comprehensive in nature, the more detailed information you can start with, the better picture you will have of what the client's experience has been to-date. Details such as plan asset base, terminations and payouts, deposit levels, etc., are all available from the plan's Form 5500. As an aside, many marketers have seized upon this fact and have begun to sell this data, which they obtain under the Freedom of Information Act. A prospect's commitment level to your process, and potential role in becoming their new plan advisor, is often gauged by how responsive they are to the data request.

FIGURE 15.4

NEW CO, Inc.

DEFINED CONTRIBUTION/401(k) ADMINISTRATIVE SUMMARY

Basic Administrative Services

Preparation of Form 5500 (R or C).

Reconciliation of data.

Reconciliation of plan assets.

Reconciliation of assets to individual accounts.

Allocation of earnings and forfeitures to individual accounts.

Calculation of safe-harbor minimum.

Recordkeeping with regard to salary deferrals, allocation to investment option (monthly).

Allocation of matching contribution, according to matching formula.

Allocation of Profit Sharing contribution according to new comp allocation formula.

Discrimination testing for matching deposits and contributions (401(k) plans).

Preparation of employee benefit statements.

Determination of highly & non-highly compensated employees.

Unlimited investment options per person (self-directed accounts).

Receipt of data on magnetic tape or disc.

Recordkeeping regarding maximum salary deferral measured against dollar limitation (401(k) plans).

	Annual
Base Fee – Both Plans	$ 1,500
Per Participating Employee	$ 30
Terminations/Loans	$ 75
First Year Only	
Installation Fee	$ 250
Trust Document preparation fee	$100 - $1,500

FIGURE 15.5

Plan Takeover Checklist

__ 1. Copy of plan document, including amendments.
(If Prototype plan, copy of adoption agreement and underlying plan document).

__ 2. Copy of IRS determination letter (Opinion letter if prototype plan).

__ 3. Copy of investment contract (Annuity or group annuity contract).

__ 4. Copy of the Form 5500 (and all applicable schedules) from previous plan year.

__ 5. Listing of individual participant's account balances, isolated by contribution source   (i.e. elective deferrals, matching contributions, safe harbor contributions, qualified non-elective contributions (QNECs), qualified matching contributions (QMACs), profit sharing; rollover).

__ 6. Loan schedules, including initial loan amount, outstanding loan balance, term of loan, interest rate, frequency of payments, periodic payment.

__ 7. Results of prior year discrimination test (ADP, ACP, general non-discrimination test, if applicable).

__ 8. History of elective deferral contributions (and account balance as of December 31, 1988 if available).

__ 9. Copy of beneficiary designation forms (including spousal waiver forms, if applicable).

Huh?

A final word on listening. As with most consultative relationships, listening is a precious commodity. The ability to hear and understand what the clients have and how they feel about their existing plan, as well as what they would prefer to achieve with it, is the most significant step towards creating a solid relationship. Only by comprehending what it takes to make someone else's client happy can we hope to improve their situation enough that they not only become our client, but our happy client.

Appendix A

Historical Elective Deferral Limits

The dollar limit on salary deferrals to a 401(k) plan was first implemented by the addition of Section 402(g) to the Internal Revenue Code by the Tax Reform Act of 1986. The initial limit was $7,000 for the 1987 calendar year, with scheduled increases for inflation indexing.

In 1994 the Uruguay Round Agreements Act (URAA '94) rounded the inflation adjustments so that increases would be made only in increments of $500.

In 2001, the Economic Growth and Tax Reconciliation Relief Act implemented a schedule of more significant increases to the ceiling for 2002 through 2006, and added a catch-up contribution provision for individuals who are age 50 or over. (Note that lower limits apply in the case of a SIMPLE 401(k) plan—see Chapter 5.)

The historical limits since 1986 are shown in Figure A.1:

FIGURE A.1	Elective Deferral Limit	Catch-up Contribution	Total (age 50 or over)
2006	$15,000	$5,000	$20,000
2005	14,000	4,000	18,000
2004	13,000	3,000	16,000
2003	12,000	2,000	14,000
2002	11,000	1,000	12,000
2001	10,500	N/A	10,500
2000	10,500	N/A	10,500
1999	10,000	N/A	10,000
1998	10,000	N/A	10,000
1997	9,500	N/A	9,500
1996	9,500	N/A	9,500
1995	9,240	N/A	9,240
1994	9,240	N/A	9,240
1993	8,994	N/A	8,994
1992	8,728	N/A	8,728
1991	8,475	N/A	8,475
1990	7,979	N/A	7,979
1989	7,627	N/A	7,627
1988	7,313	N/A	7,313
1987	7,000	N/A	7,000

Appendix  B

Sample Plan Document

ADOPTION AGREEMENT 004 TO

THE FAIR, AUFSESSER & FITZGERALD, P.C. DEFINED CONTRIBUTION PROTOTYPE PLAN AND TRUST AGREEMENT

FOR A NONSTANDARDIZED PROFIT SHARING AND/OR 401(K) PLAN

NAME OF EMPLOYER   SPECIMEN FOR *THE 401(k) ADVISOR*

ADDRESS   123 Savings Lane
Futureville, Alaska

NAME OF PLAN   THE ULTIMATE 401(k) ADVISOR PLAN

NAME OF
COMMITTEE MEMBERS   SEYMOUR MONEY

INTRODUCTION

This Adoption Agreement and the provisions of The Fair, Aufsesser & FitzGerald, P.C. Defined Contribution Prototype Plan and Trust Agreement of which this Agreement is a part, are hereby adopted by the Employer or Employers executing this Agreement for the benefit of Employees and their Beneficiaries.

Complete (A), (B), (C) or (D) below:

_____ (A) This Adoption Agreement is part of the adoption of a new Plan.

_____ (B) This Adoption Agreement is a restatement of a previously adopted Plan, other than The Fair, Aufsesser & FitzGerald, P.C. Defined Contribution Prototype Plan, as provided in Section 12.06.

_____ (C) This Adoption Agreement is a restatement of a Fair, Aufsesser & FitzGerald, P.C. Defined Contribution Prototype Plan.

Complete only Items amended

_____ (D) This Adoption Agreement is an amendment to The Fair, Aufsesser & FitzGerald, P.C. Defined Contribution Prototype Plan, previously adopted, as provided in Section 12.02.

The Plan Administrator shall be [select one]

__X__ the Committee.

_____ the Employer.

_____ the following individuals: [insert names]

_____.

Item 1: EFFECTIVE DATE

Effective Date shall mean [insert date] January 1, 2005.

If this Agreement is a restatement of a previously adopted plan, the Effective Date of the previously adopted Plan is [insert date]

Item 2: ELIGIBLE EMPLOYEE

A. An Eligible Employee shall be any Employee who satisfies the eligibility conditions set forth in Item 3. If elected in this Item, the term "Eligible Employee" shall include [check only if Employees in the listed category are to be included]

_____ any Employee who is a member of a unit of Employees covered by a collective bargaining agreement with an Employee representative if the Employer and the Employee representative have engaged in good faith bargaining for retirement benefits, and if less than two (2%) percent of the Employees of the Employer who are covered pursuant to that agreement are professionals as defined in section 1.410(b)-9(g) of the proposed Income Tax Regulations. The term "Employee representative" shall not include any organization more than half of whose members are Employees who are owners, officers or executives of the Employer.

_____ any Employee who is a nonresident alien provided the Employee receives no earned income from the Employer, within the meaning of section 911(d)(2) of the Code, which constitutes income from sources within the United States within the meaning of section 861(a)(3) of the Code.

_____ any Employee who became an Employee as the result of a section 410(b)(6)(C) transaction. These Employees will be excluded during the period beginning on the date of the transaction and ending on the last day of the first Plan Year beginning after the date of the transaction. A section 410(b)(6)(C) transaction is an asset or stock acquisition, merger, or similar transaction involving a change in the Employer of the Employees of a trade or business.

B.   The term "Eligible Employee" shall include [select one]

__X__ only Employees employed by an Employer adopting the Plan.

_____ all Employees required to be aggregated under section 414(b), (c) or (m) of the Code, and any individual deemed under section 414(n) or section 414(o) of the Code to be an Employee of any Employer adopting the Plan.

C.   If elected in this Item, the term "Eligible Employee" shall exclude [check only if Employees in the category are to be excluded]

_____ Employees compensated on a salaried basis.

_____ Employees who are hourly paid.

_____ Employees who are paid solely on a commission basis.

_____ Employees who are paid partially on a commission basis.

D. The term "Eligible Employee" shall exclude the following Employees: [insert specific identification of excluded employees, e.g. job classification, geographic location, etc.] _____.

Item 3: ELIGIBILITY CONDITIONS

A.1. ENTRY DATE: FOR NON-QUALIFIED EMPLOYER CONTRIBUTIONS OR QUALIFIED NON-ELECTIVE CONTRIBUTIONS an Employee who qualifies as an Eligible Employee under Item 2 shall be eligible to participate on the earlier of the first day of the Plan Year beginning after the date on which the Employee has met the minimum Age and service requirements, six (6) months after the date such requirements are met, or an Entry Date determined as follows: [select one]

____X__ the Entry Date shall be the first day of the Plan Year.

_____ the Entry Date shall be _____ [insert month and day] in each Plan Year.

_____ the Entry Date shall be twice each Plan Year, on the first day of the Plan Year and six months following the first day of the Plan Year.

_____ the Entry Date shall be twice each Plan Year, on _____ [insert month and day] and six months after such date.

_____ the Entry Date shall be the first day of the month coincident with or next following the Employee's completion of the eligibility requirements selected in this Item 3.

_____ the Entry Date shall be the day the Employee completes his or her first Hour of Service.

_____ the Entry Date shall be the first day of the sixth month following the day the Employee completes his or her first Hour of Service.

_____ [insert date or series of dates - quarterly, monthly, daily or special first year Entry Date] _____.

A.2. ENTRY DATE: FOR ELECTIVE DEFERRALS AND MATCHING CON-TRIBUTIONS: an Employee who qualifies as an Eligible Employee under Item 2 shall be eligible to participate on the earlier of the first day of the Plan Year beginning after the date on which the Employee has met the minimum Age and service requirements, six (6) months after the date such requirements are met, or an Entry Date determined as follows: [select one]

__X__ the Entry Date shall be the first day of the Plan Year.

_____ the Entry Date shall be _____ [insert month and day] in each Plan Year.

_____ the Entry Date shall be twice each Plan Year, on the first day of the Plan Year and six months following the first day of the Plan Year.

_____ the Entry Date shall be twice each Plan Year, on _____ [insert month and day] and six months after such date.

_____ the Entry Date shall be the first day of the month coincident with or next following the Employee's completion of the eligibility require-ments selected in this Item 3.

_____ the Entry Date shall be the day the Employee completes his or her first Hour of Service.

_____ the Entry Date shall be the first day of the sixth month follow-ing the day the Employee completes his or her first Hour of Service.

_____ [insert date or series of dates - quarterly, monthly, daily or special first year Entry Date] _____.

B.   AGE REQUIREMENT: An Employee who qualifies as an Eligible Employee under Item 2 shall be eligible to participate on the Effective Date only if he or she has attained Age __21__. [do not insert Age above 21]

An Eligible Employee shall be eligible to participate after the Effective Date only if as of an Entry Date he or she has attained Age __21__. [do not insert Age above 21]

An Employee's Age shall be his or her Age [select one]

___X___ on his or her last birthday.

_____ on his or her nearest birthday.

C.1. SERVICE REQUIREMENT FOR NON-QUALIFIED EMPLOYER CON-TRIBUTIONS OR QUALIFIED NON-ELECTIVE CONTRIBUTIONS: An Employee who qualifies as an Eligible Employee under Item 2 shall be eligible to participate for Non-Qualified Employer Contributions or Qualified Non-Elective Contributions on the Effective Date only if he or she has completed [select one]

___1___ Years of Service. [do not insert more than one year unless all Participants are immediately fully vested; do not insert more than two years in any event]

_____ months of service. [use only if Elapsed Time Rule is elected; do not insert more than twelve months unless all Participants are immediately fully vested; do not insert more than twenty-four (24) months in any event]

An Eligible Employee shall be eligible to participate for Non-Qualified Employer Contributions or Qualified Non-Elective Contributions after the Effective Date only if as of an Entry Date he or she has completed [select one]

___1___ Years of Service. [do not insert more than one year unless all Participants are immediately fully vested; do not insert more than two years in any event]

_____ months of service. [use only if Elapsed Time Rule is elected; do not insert more than twelve months unless all Participants are immediately fully vested; do not insert more than twenty-four (24) months in any event]

C.2. SERVICE REQUIREMENT FOR ELECTIVE DEFERRALS AND MATCHING CONTRIBUTIONS: An Employee who qualifies as an Eligible Employee under Item 2 shall be eligible to participate for Elective Deferrals and Matching Contributions on the Effective Date only if he or she has completed [select one]

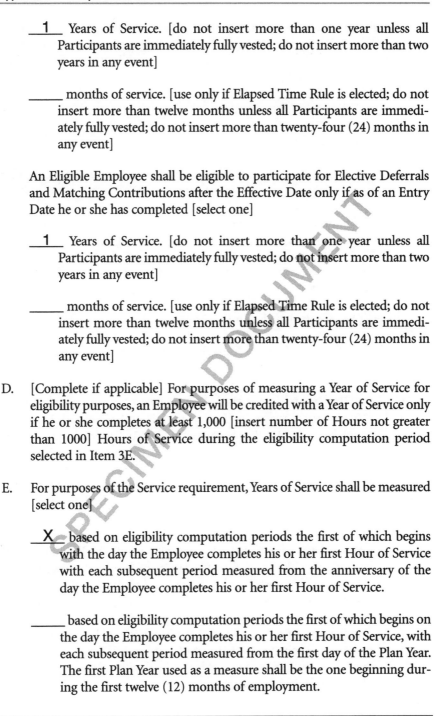

___1___ Years of Service. [do not insert more than one year unless all Participants are immediately fully vested; do not insert more than two years in any event]

_____ months of service. [use only if Elapsed Time Rule is elected; do not insert more than twelve months unless all Participants are immediately fully vested; do not insert more than twenty-four (24) months in any event]

An Eligible Employee shall be eligible to participate for Elective Deferrals and Matching Contributions after the Effective Date only if as of an Entry Date he or she has completed [select one]

___1___ Years of Service. [do not insert more than one year unless all Participants are immediately fully vested; do not insert more than two years in any event]

_____ months of service. [use only if Elapsed Time Rule is elected; do not insert more than twelve months unless all Participants are immediately fully vested; do not insert more than twenty-four (24) months in any event]

D.   [Complete if applicable] For purposes of measuring a Year of Service for eligibility purposes, an Employee will be credited with a Year of Service only if he or she completes at least 1,000 [insert number of Hours not greater than 1000] Hours of Service during the eligibility computation period selected in Item 3E.

E.   For purposes of the Service requirement, Years of Service shall be measured [select one]

___X___ based on eligibility computation periods the first of which begins with the day the Employee completes his or her first Hour of Service with each subsequent period measured from the anniversary of the day the Employee completes his or her first Hour of Service.

_____ based on eligibility computation periods the first of which begins on the day the Employee completes his or her first Hour of Service, with each subsequent period measured from the first day of the Plan Year. The first Plan Year used as a measure shall be the one beginning during the first twelve (12) months of employment.

F. For all purposes under this Plan, Years of Service as a Proprietor or with a predecessor Partnership, Years of Service with a corporate predecessor, or Years of Service with the employer named below [check one if applicable, otherwise leave blank]

_____ shall be taken into account.

_____ shall not be taken into account.

_____ shall be taken into account only for Years of Service completed after _____ (insert date).

If Years of Service with a predecessor are to be counted, the name of the predecessor is _____.

If Years of Service with an unrelated employer are to be counted, the name of such employer is _____.

G. Years of Service shall be determined [select one]

X on the basis of actual Hours for which an Employee is paid or entitled to payment.

_____ on the basis of days worked. An Employee shall be credited with ten (10) Hours of Service if under Section 1.41 of the Plan such Employee would be credited with at least one (1) Hour of Service during the day.

_____ on the basis of weeks worked. An Employee shall be credited with forty-five (45) Hours of Service if under Section 1.41 of the Plan such Employee would be credited with at least one (1) Hour of Service during the week.

_____ on the basis of semi-monthly payroll periods. An Employee shall be credited with ninety-five (95) Hours of Service if under Section 1.41 of the Plan such Employee would be credited with at least one (1) Hour of Service during the semi-monthly payroll period.

_____ on the basis of months worked. An Employee shall be credited with one hundred ninety (190) Hours of Service if under Section 1.41 of the Plan such Employee would be credited with at least one (1) Hour of Service during the month.

_____ on the basis of the Elapsed Time Rule set forth in Section 2.09. If the Elapsed Time Rule is selected, it shall be applied for purposes of determining [check applicable boxes]

_____ the eligibility computation period.

_____ the accrual computation period.

_____ the vesting computation period.

_____ the Participant's Normal Retirement Age.

_____ Years of Service or Participation for benefit determinations under the Plan benefit formula.

_____ Years of Service and Participation for all purposes under the Plan.

H.   Hours of Service [select one]

_____ shall

__X__ shall not

be credited for periods prior to the date an employer was part of an affiliated service group, controlled group of corporations, or a group of trades or businesses under common control with a participating Employer. If such Hours of Service shall be credited,

_____ all Hours of Service with such employer

_____ Hours of Service with such employer after _____ shall be counted.   [insert date]

Item 4: COMPENSATION

A.   Compensation for a Plan Year shall mean [select one]

__X__ Compensation as defined in Section 8.05(b)(1) of the Plan.

_____ section 3401(a) wages.

_____ 415 safe harbor Compensation.

B. Employer contributions made pursuant to a salary reduction agreement which are not includible in the gross income of the Employee under [check where applicable]

__X__ section 125,

__X__ section 402(e)(3),

__X__ section 402(h)(1)(B), or

__X__ section 403(b)

of the Code [select one]

__X__ shall

_____ shall not

be included as Compensation for Plan purposes.

C. Compensation shall not include [check only if indicated type of Compensation is to be excluded]

_____ overtime.

_____ bonuses.

_____ commissions.

_____ bonuses paid to Highly Compensated Employees.

_____ commissions paid to Highly Compensated Employees.

_____ bonuses paid to stockholders and owners of the Employer.

_____ Compensation earned by a Participant prior to his or her Entry Date.

_____ [insert exclusion] _____.

D. Compensation for purposes of determining Employer contributions shall be measured over a twelve (12) consecutive month period [select one]

_____ measured by the Plan Year beginning in the fiscal year of the Employer.

_____ measured by the Plan Year ending in the fiscal year of the Employer.

_____ measured by the calendar year beginning in the fiscal year of the Employer.

_____ measured by the calendar year ending in the fiscal year of the Employer.

X measured by the fiscal year of the Employer [select one]

_____ ending immediately prior to

X ending during

the Plan Year for which the determination is made.

_____ measured by the calendar year [select one]

_____ ending immediately prior to

_____ ending during

the Plan Year for which the determination is made.

_____ beginning with each _____ [insert month and day].

NOTE: No selection shall be made under this Item 4D unless the measuring period selected ends with or within the Plan Year.

E. If the Compensation of a Highly Compensated Employee and certain Family Members was limited by the provisions of section 414(q)(6) of the Code, that limitation for any Plan purposes: [complete as applicable]

_____ ceased to apply in the Plan Year beginning in 1997.

_____ ceased to apply in the Plan Year beginning in 1998.

_____ ceased to apply in the Plan Year beginning in 1999.

X is not applicable.

F.   Highly Compensated Employees

_____ In determining who is a Highly Compensated Employee, they are 5-percent owners and others after the Employer makes a Top Paid Group election. The effect of this election is that an Employee (who is not a 5-percent owner at any time during the determination year or the Look-Back Year) with Compensation in excess of Eighty Thousand ($80,000) Dollars (as adjusted) for the Look-Back Year is a Highly Compensated Employee only if the Employee was in the Top-Paid Group for the Look-Back Year. This election shall first apply on [insert date] _____.

_____ In determining who is a Highly Compensated Employee (other than as a 5-percent owner) the Employer makes a calendar year data election. The effect of this election is that the Look-Back Year is the calendar year beginning with or within the Look-Back Year.

_____ If the definition is limited to the Top-Paid Group, such election first applied to the Plan Year beginning in _____[insert Plan Year].

Item 5: NORMAL AND EARLY RETIREMENT AGE

A.   Normal Retirement Age shall mean [select one]

_____ the day and month of the Participant's _____ [insert Age not later than 65] birthday.

__X__ the later of the day on which the Participant attains Age _65_ [insert Age no later than 65] or the _5th_ [insert number no greater than 5] anniversary of the Participation Commencement Date.

_____ the later of the day on which the Participant attains Age _____ [insert Age no later than 65] or the Anniversary Date following his or her completion of ____ Years of Service, but in no event later than the Participant's attainment of Age sixty-five (65).

_____ the later of the day on which the Participant attains Age _____ [insert Age no later than 65] or the Anniversary Date following his or her completion of ____ Years of Service, but in no event later than the later of the Participant's attainment of Age sixty-five (65) or the fifth (5th) anniversary of the Participation Commencement Date.

_____ the day on which the Participant attains Age _____ [insert Age no later than 65] and completes _____ Years of Service, but in no event later than the Participant's attainment of Age sixty-five (65).

_____ the day on which the Participant attains Age _____ [insert Age no later than 65] and completes _____ Years of Service, but in no event later than the later of the Participant's attainment of Age sixty-five (65) or the fifth (5th) anniversary of the Participation Commencement Date.

_____ the day on which the Participant attains Age _____ [insert Age no later than 65] and completes _____ Years of Participation, but in no event later than the Participant's attainment of Age sixty-five (65).

_____ the day on which the Participant attains Age _____ [insert Age no later than 65] and completes _____ Years of Participation, but in no event later than the later of the Participant's attainment of Age sixty-five (65) or the fifth (5th) anniversary of the Participation Commencement Date.

_____ the day on which the Participant attains Age _____ [insert Age no later than 65], completes _____ Years of Service, and completes _____ Years of Participation, but in no event later than the Participant's attainment of Age sixty-five (65).

_____ the day on which the Participant attains Age _____ [insert Age no later than 65], completes _____ Years of Service, and completes _____ Years of Participation, but in no event later than the later of the Participant's attainment of Age sixty-five (65) or the fifth (5th) anniversary of the Participation Commencement Date.

_____ [check if applicable] if, for Plan Years beginning before January 1, 1988, a Participant's Normal Retirement Age was determined with reference to an anniversary of his or her Participation Commencement Date that was more than five (5) but no greater than ten (10) years, and an anniversary of the Participation Commencement Date is relevant in determining a Participant's Normal Retirement Age, the anniversary of a Participant's

Participation Commencement Date used to determine the Participant's Normal Retirement Age for a Participant who first commenced participation under the Plan before the first Plan Year beginning on or after January 1, 1988, shall be the earlier of the tenth (10th) anniversary of the Participant's Participation Commencement Date (or the anniversary set forth in the Plan as applicable prior to that Plan Year) or the fifth (5th) anniversary of the first day of the first Plan Year beginning on or after January 1, 1988.

If Years of Service are a factor in determining a Participant's Normal Retirement Age, Years of Service for such purpose shall be measured over [select one]

_____ the Plan Year.

_____ the twelve (12) consecutive month periods measured from the date the Participant performs his or her first Hour of Service and each anniversary thereof.

_____ the twelve (12) consecutive month period measured from each _____ [insert month and day].

_____ over the eligibility computation period selected in Item 3E.

B.   Normal Retirement Date shall mean the [select one]

_____ first day of the Plan Year in which the Participant's Normal Retirement Age occurs.

_____ last day of the Plan Year in which the Participant's Normal Retirement Age occurs.

__X__ first day of the Plan Year nearest the Participant's Normal Retirement Age.

_____ last day of the Plan Year nearest the Participant's Normal Retirement Age.

_____ the Participant's Normal Retirement Age.

_____ the first day of the month coincident with or next following the Participant's Normal Retirement Age.

_____ the Valuation Date coincident with or next following the Participant's Normal Retirement Age.

No selection made under this Item 5B shall cause benefits to be distributable later than the latest date determined under Section 4.03 of the Plan.

C.   Early Retirement Date shall mean any date after [select one]

_____ the day and month of the Participant's _____ [insert Age] birthday.

_____ the later of the day on which the Participant attains Age _____ [insert Age] or the _____ [insert number] anniversary of the Participation Commencement Date.

_____ the later of the day on which the Participant attains Age _____ [insert Age] or the Anniversary Date following his or her completion of _____ [insert number] Years of Service.

_____ the day on which the Participant attains Age _____ [insert Age], completes _____ [insert number] Years of Service, and completes [insert number] Years of Participation.

Item 6: DISABILITY PROVISION [select one]

A.   The Accrued Benefit of a Participant

__X__ shall be fully vested on disability in accordance with Section 5.02.

_____ in the event of his or her disability will be vested and distribution rights will be the same as the vesting and distribution rights applicable on his or her termination of employment.

B.   A Participant who makes Elective Deferrals [select one]

__X__ shall

_____ shall not

receive the value of his Accrued Benefit on his Disability Date.

C.   Contributions for a Disabled Participant who is not a Highly Compensated Employee [select one]

__X__ shall

_____ shall not

be made during the period of Disability in accordance with the provisions of Section 5.03. If contributions are to be made in accordance with the preceding sentence, Item 15 must provide that all Participants shall be fully vested at all times.

Item 7: EMPLOYER CONTRIBUTION

A.   This Plan [select one]

__X__ shall

_____ shall not

include a cash or deferred arrangement.

The provisions of a cash or deferred arrangement may be made effective as of the first day of the Plan Year in which the cash or deferred arrangement is adopted. However, under no circumstances may a Salary Reduction Agreement or other deferral mechanism be adopted retroactively.

B.   The Employer shall contribute [select one]

__X__ the amount determined each year by its governing body.

_____% [insert percentage] of each Participant's Compensation.

_____% [insert percentage] of the Employer's Net Profits for the fiscal year ending with or within the Plan Year in excess of $_____.

_____ no contribution.

The Employer contribution shall be made [select one]

__X__ whether or not the Employer has Net Profits for the year.

_____ only if the Employer has Net Profits for the year.

The Employer contribution shall be allocated [select one]

__X__ to all Eligible Employees, whether or not the Employee has executed a Salary Reduction Agreement.

_____ only to those Employees who have executed a Salary Reduction Agreement.

If the Employer shall make Matching Contributions, such contributions shall not be made for the following classes of Eligible Employees:

_____ Highly Compensated Employees.

_____ five (5%) percent owners of the Employer.

_____ [describe excluded class] _____.

C.   If the Employer shall make contributions, such contributions may include [check applicable selections]

__X__ Matching Contributions.

__X__ Qualified Non-elective Contributions.

__X__ Non-Qualified Employer Contributions.

C.1 If the Employer shall make Matching Contributions, such contributions shall be [select one]

_____ Qualified Matching Contributions at all times.

__X__ Qualified Matching Contributions only if, at the time the contribution is made, the Employer advises the Committee that such contributions are Qualified Matching Contributions; otherwise, such contributions shall be Non-Qualified Matching Contributions.

_____ Non-Qualified Matching Contributions.

C.2. If the Employer shall make contributions other than Matching Contributions, such contributions shall be [select one]

_____ Qualified Non-elective Contributions at all times.

__X__ Qualified Non-elective Contributions only if, at the time the contribution is made, the Employer advises the Committee that such contributions are Qualified Non-elective Contributions; otherwise such contributions shall be Non-Qualified Employer Contributions.

_____ Non-Qualified Employer Contributions.

C.3. If the Employer shall make Matching Contributions, such contributions [select one]

C.3.a. __X__ shall be determined to be Matching Contributions only if, at the time the contribution is made, the Employer advises the Committee that such contributions are Matching Contributions, in which event such contributions shall be allocated to the Account of each Participant in accordance with the Elective Deferrals of such Participant for the Plan Year for which the Matching Contribution is made.

C.3.b. _____ shall equal _____% [insert percentage] of the Elective Deferrals of each Participant for the Plan Year, but in no event shall the Matching Contribution be greater than _____% [insert percentage, if applicable] of the Participant's Compensation determined for the Plan Year by the Employer.

C.3.c. _____ shall equal [select applicable items]

_____% [insert percentage] of the Elective Deferrals of each Participant for the Plan Year up to _____% [insert percentage] of the Participant's Compensation,

_____% [insert percentage] of the next _____% [insert percentage] of the Elective Deferrals of each Participant for the Plan Year up to _____% [insert percentage] of the Participant's Compensation, and

_____% [insert percentage] of the next _____% [insert percentage] of the Elective Deferrals of each Participant for the Plan Year up to _____% [insert percentage] of the Participant's Compensation.

C.3.d. _____ shall be equal to the percentage of Elective Deferrals of a Participant based on his Compensation for the Plan Year as follows: [select one if applicable]

> _____% [insert percentage] if his Compensation is less than $_____; [insert dollar amount]

> _____% [insert percentage] if his Compensation is more than the dollar amount chosen in the preceding selection, but less than $_____; [insert dollar amount]

> _____% [insert percentage] if his Compensation is more than the dollar amount chosen in the preceding selection, but less than $_____; [insert dollar amount]

> _____% [insert percentage] if his Compensation is more than the dollar amount chosen in the preceding selection.

C.3.e. _____ shall be equal to the percentage of Elective Deferrals of a Participant based on his [select one]

> _____ Years of Service

> _____ Years of Participation

as of the last day of the Plan Year as follows: [select one if applicable]

> _____% [insert percentage] if the number of Years is less than _____ [insert number of Years];

> _____% [insert percentage] if the number of Years is more than the number of Years chosen in the preceding selection, but less than _____ [insert number of Years];

> _____% [insert percentage] if the number of Years is more than the number of Years chosen in the preceding selection.

C.3. f. _____ [Check if Applicable] This formula shall apply to the following group(s) of Employees only: [insert group(s)] _____.

If groups are listed in Item 7.C.3.f. above, Item 7.C.4. shall apply to all other Participants. [If Item 7.C.3.f. is completed Item 7.C.4. must also be completed.]

C.4. If the Employer shall make Matching Contributions, such contributions [select one]

C.4.a. _____ shall be determined to be Matching Contributions only if, at the time the contribution is made, the Employer advises the Committee that such contributions are Matching Contributions, in which event such contributions shall be allocated to the Account of each Participant in accordance with the Elective Deferrals of such Participant for the Plan Year for which the Matching Contribution is made.

C.4.b. _____ shall equal _____% [insert percentage] of the Elective Deferrals of each Participant for the Plan Year, but in no event shall the Matching Contribution be greater than _____% [insert percentage, if applicable] of the Participant's Compensation determined for the Plan Year by the Employer.

C.4.c. _____ shall equal [select applicable items]

> _____% [insert percentage] of the Elective Deferrals of each Participant for the Plan Year up to _____% [insert percentage] of the Participant's Compensation,

> _____% [insert percentage] of the next _____% [insert percentage] of the Elective Deferrals of each Participant for the Plan Year up to _____% [insert percentage] of the Participant's Compensation, and

> _____% [insert percentage] of the next _____% [insert percentage] of the Elective Deferrals of each Participant for the Plan Year up to _____% [insert percentage] of the Participant's Compensation.

C.4.d. _____ shall be equal to the percentage of Elective Deferrals of a Participant based on his Compensation for the Plan Year as follows: [select one if applicable]

> _____% [insert percentage] if his Compensation is less than $_____; [insert dollar amount]

_____% [insert percentage] if his Compensation is more than the dollar amount chosen in the preceding selection, but less than $_____; [insert dollar amount]

_____% [insert percentage] if his Compensation is more than the dollar amount chosen in the preceding selection, but less than $_____; [insert dollar amount]

_____% [insert percentage] if his Compensation is more than the dollar amount chosen in the preceding selection.

C.4.e.   _____ shall be equal to the percentage of Elective Deferrals of a Participant based on his [select one]

_____ Years of Service

_____ Years of Participation

as of the last day of the Plan Year as follows: [select one if applicable]

_____% [insert percentage] if the number of Years is less than _____ [insert number of Years];

_____% [insert percentage] if the number of Years is more than the number of Years chosen in the preceding selection, but less than _____ [insert number of Years];

_____% [insert percentage] if the number of Years is more than the number of Years chosen in the preceding selection.

C.5. If Matching Contributions are limited by Compensation, Compensation for the purpose of measuring the limitation shall be

__X__ annual Compensation.

_____ Compensation paid during each pay period separately determined.

_____ the rate of Compensation paid on the first day of the Plan Year.

_____ annual Compensation credited during the prior Plan Year.

C.6. If the Employer shall make Matching Contributions which are not qualified, such contributions shall be [select one]

　X　 vested in accordance with the applicable schedule elected under
　　　Item 15.

_____ fully vested at all times.

_____ vested in accordance with the following schedule, but subject to
the schedule set forth in Item 15A if the Plan is a Top-Heavy
Plan.

　　_____% [insert any percentage not less than zero] after one (1) Year
　　of Service;

　　_____% [insert any percentage not less than zero] after two (2) Years
　　of Service;

　　_____% [not less than 20%] after three (3) Years of Service;

　　_____% [not less than 40%] after four (4) Years of Service;

　　_____% [not less than 60%] after five (5) Years of Service;

　　_____% [not less than 80%] after six (6) Years of Service;

100% after seven (7) Years of Service.

C.7. In no event shall the Matching Contribution for any Employee exceed
[complete if applicable]

$_____.

_____% of the Participant's Compensation.

_____% of the Elective Deferral of the Participant.

C.8. In determining Elective Deferrals for the purpose of the Average Deferral
Percentage test

_____ all Qualified Matching Contributions

__X__ such Qualified Matching Contributions as are needed to meet the Actual Deferral Percentage test

_____ all Qualified Non-elective Contributions

__X__ such Qualified Non-elective Contributions as are needed to meet the Actual Deferral Percentage test

shall be taken into account.

D.1. Qualified Non-elective Contributions, if permitted, [select one, if applicable]

__X__ shall

_____ shall not

be included in the Contribution Percentage Amounts.

The amount of Qualified Non-elective Contributions to be taken into account as Contribution Percentage Amounts shall be

_____ all Qualified Non-elective Contributions.

__X__ such Qualified Non-elective Contributions as are needed to meet the Average Contribution Percentage test set forth in Section 7.12 of the Plan.

D.2. Elective Deferrals, if permitted, [select one, if applicable]

_____ shall

__X__ shall not

be included in the Contribution Percentage Amounts.

The amount of Elective Deferrals to be taken into account as Contribution Percentage Amounts shall be

_____ all Elective Deferrals.

_____ such Elective Deferrals as are needed to meet the Average Contribution Percentage test set forth in Section 7.12 of the Plan.

E.1. _____ If this is not a successor plan, then, if checked, for the first Plan Year this Plan permits any Participant to make Employee Contributions, provides for Matching Contributions or both, the ACP used in the ACP test for Participants who are non-Highly Compensated Employee shall be such first Plan Year's ACP. (Do not check this box if the Employer has elected in the Adoption Agreement to use the Current Year Testing method.)

E.2. _____ If checked, this Plan is using the Current Year Testing method for purposes of the ADP and ACP tests. (This box cannot be "unchecked" for a Plan Year unless (1) the Plan has been using the Current Year Testing method for the preceding five (5) Plan Years, or, if lesser, the number of Plan Years the Plan has been in existence; or (2) the Plan otherwise meets one of the conditions specified in Notice 98-1 (or superseding guidance) for changing from the current year testing method.

E.3. The Current Year Testing method was first selected in _____ [insert Plan Year].

F.1.a. Complete if Safe Harbor 401(k) is intended.

_____ Matching Contributions - Each Year, the Employer will contribute a Matching Contribution to the plan on behalf of each Employee who makes a salary reduction election under this Subsection. The amount of the Qualified Matching Contribution will be equal to the Employee's salary reduction contribution up to a limit of three (3%) percent of the Employee's Compensation for the full year plus fifty (50%) percent of the next two (2%) percent of the Employee's Compensation.

F.1.b. _____ Non-elective Contribution - For any Year, instead of a Matching Contribution, the Employer may elect to contribute a Qualified Non-elective Contribution of three (3%) percent of Compensation for the full Year for each Eligible Employee.

F.2. The Safe Harbor Contribution shall be made to: [select one]

_____ all Employees.

_____ all Non-Highly Compensated Employees.

G. If Elective Deferrals are permitted, a Participant may change the elections in his or her Salary Reduction Agreement [select one]

_____ annually, on the last day of the prior Plan Year.

_____ annually, on the first day of the Plan Year.

_____ on the last day of the sixth (6th) month of the Plan Year, and on the last day of the Plan Year.

_____ on the first day of the Plan Year, and six months following the first day of the Plan Year.

_____ on the last day of each quarter of the Plan Year.

_____ on the first day of each quarter of the Plan Year.

___X___ at such times as the Committee may determine, but no less often than once each Plan Year.

H.   If Elective Deferrals are permitted, a Participant may elect to defer up to [select one if applicable]

_____% of his or her Compensation.

_____% of his or her Compensation, up to $_____.

In no event shall a Participant be permitted to make Elective Deferrals unless the Elective Deferral selected is at least [complete if applicable]

_____% [insert percentage, if applicable] of his or her Compensation.

$_____. [insert dollar amount, if applicable]

I.   A Participant [select one]

___X___ shall

_____ shall not

be able to assign Excess Elective Deferrals to the Plan.

If the Participant can assign Excess Elective Deferrals to the Plan, such assignment must be made prior to _____ [insert month and day not later than April 15] of each year.

J.   Forfeitures of Excess Aggregate Contributions shall be [select one]

_____ reallocated to the accounts of Participants who are not Highly Compensated Employees.

_____ reallocated to the accounts of all Participants.

_____ applied to reduce Employer contributions.

__X__ applied to reduce Matching Contributions, with any excess forfeitures reallocated to Participant Accounts in the same manner as Non-Qualified Employer Contributions in the Plan Year in which the forfeiture is first recognized.

No forfeitures shall be allocated to the Account of a Participant for a Plan Year in which contributions were reduced as a result of Excess Aggregate Contributions.

K.   Forfeitures of Matching Contributions shall be [select one]

_____ reallocated to the accounts of Participants who are not Highly Compensated Employees.

_____ reallocated to the accounts of all Participants.

_____ applied to reduce Employer contributions.

__X__ applied to reduce Matching Contributions, with any excess forfeitures reallocated to Participant Accounts in the same manner as Non-Qualified Employer Contributions in the Plan Year in which the forfeiture is first recognized.

L.   All other forfeitures shall be [select one]

_____ allocated to Participant Accounts in the same manner as Non-Qualified Employer Contributions in the Plan Year in which the forfeiture is first recognized.

_____ used to reduce Non-Qualified Employer Contributions in the Plan Year in which the forfeiture is recognized. [select only if Non-Qualified Employer Contributions are required]

X first used to reduce Matching Employer Contributions in the Plan Year in which the forfeiture is recognized, then to reduce Non-Qualified Employer Contributions, and then allocated to Participant Accounts in the same manner as Non-Qualified Employer Contributions.

M. Forfeitures shall be deemed to occur [select one]

X on the last day of the Plan Year in which termination of employment occurs.

_____ on the Valuation Date coincident with or next following a Participant's termination of employment.

_____ on the last day of the Plan Year following _____ [insert number not in excess of 5] consecutive one-year Break(s) in Service for the Participant.

_____ on the Valuation Date coincident with or next following _____ [insert number not in excess of 5] consecutive one-year Break(s) in Service for the Participant.

_____ on the earlier of the last day of the Plan Year following _____ [insert number not in excess of 5] consecutive one-year Break(s) in Service for the Participant or the last day of the Plan Year in which the Participant's vested benefit is distributed.

A forfeiture cannot be allocated prior to the Valuation Date coincident with or next following a Participant's fifth (5th) consecutive one-year Break in Service unless a distribution has been made to the Participant.

N. Forfeitures

_____ shall

_____ shall not

be allocated to Participants who first enter the Plan in the Plan Year for which the forfeiture is allocated.

Item 8: ALLOCATION OF CONTRIBUTIONS

A.   Employer contributions, other than Matching Contributions, shall be allocated [select one]

   X   to each Participant in the same proportion as his or her Compensation bears to the Compensation of all Participants.

_____ on an integrated basis.

If Employer contributions are to be allocated on an integrated basis, Qualified Non-elective Contributions

_____ shall

_____ shall not

be included.

B.   If Employer contributions other than Matching Contributions or Elective Deferrals are to be allocated on an integrated basis, the percentage of Compensation in excess of the Integration Level shall be [select one]

_____% [insert percentage not greater than 5.7% if the Integration Level is the Taxable Wage Base, less than 20% of the Taxable Wage Base or $10,000; insert percentage not greater than 5.4% if the Integration Level is more than 80% of the Taxable Wage Base but less than the Taxable Wage Base; insert percentage not greater than 4.3% if the Integration Level is more than $10,000 and more than 20% of the Taxable Wage Base but less than 80% of the Taxable Wage Base].

_____ 4.3% if the Integration Level is more than $10,000 and more than 20% of the Taxable Wage Base but less than 80% of the Taxable Wage Base for the Year, 5.4% if the Integration Level is more than 80% of the Taxable Wage Base but less than the Taxable Wage Base, and 5.7% if the Integration Level is either $10,000, 20% of the Taxable Wage Base or the Taxable Wage Base.

_____% [insert percentage which satisfies the general test under the provisions of the Income Tax Regulations issued under section 401(a)(4) of the Code]

The Integration Level shall be [select one]

_____ the Taxable Wage Base.

$_____ [insert dollar amount less than the Taxable Wage Base]

_____% of the Taxable Wage Base [insert percentage not in excess of 100%]

C.1.   Non-Qualified Employer Contributions shall be allocated to Participant Accounts as of an Allocation Date, which shall be [select one]

___X___ the last day of the Plan Year.

_____ the first day of the Plan Year.

_____ the following date or dates in each Plan Year:

_____ [insert date(s)].

Subject to the provisions of Section 2.10, and the election set forth in Item 15E, an allocation of Non-Qualified Employer Contributions [select one]

_____ shall

___X___ shall not

be made to the Account of a Participant who completes less than 1,000 (insert number of hours not to exceed 1,000 Hours) Hours of Service during the Plan Year.

Subject to the provisions of Section 2.10, an allocation of Non-Qualified Employer Contributions [select one]

_____ shall

___X___ shall not

be made to the account of a Participant who is not employed on the [select one]

_____ Allocation Date.

___X___ last day of the Plan Year.

C.2. Qualified Non-elective Contributions shall be allocated to Participant Accounts as of an Allocation Date, which shall be [select one]

   X   the last day of the Plan Year.

_____ the first day of the Plan Year.

_____ the following date or dates in each Plan Year:

_____ [insert date(s)].

Qualified Non-elective Contributions

_____ shall

_____ shall not

be allocated to non-Highly Compensated Employees.

Subject to the provisions of Section 2.10, and the election set forth in Item 15E, an allocation of Qualified Non-elective Contributions [select one]

_____ shall

   X   shall not

be made to the Account of a Participant who completes less than 1,000(insert number of hours not to exceed 1,000 Hours) Hours of Service during the Plan Year.

Subject to the provisions of Section 2.10, an allocation of Qualified Non-elective Contributions [select one]

_____ shall

   X   shall not

be made to the account of a Participant who is not employed on the last day of the Plan Year.

C.3. Matching Contributions shall be allocated to Participant Accounts as of an Allocation Date, which shall be [select one]

__X__ the last day of the Plan Year.

_____ the first day of the Plan Year.

_____ the date each Elective Deferral is allocated.

_____ the following date or dates in each Plan Year:

_____ [insert date(s)].

Subject to the provisions of Section 2.10, and the election set forth in Item 15E, an allocation of Matching Contributions [select one]

_____ shall

__X__ shall not

be made to the Account of a Participant who completes less than 1,000(insert number of hours not to exceed 1,000 Hours) Hours of Service during the Plan Year.

Subject to the provisions of Section 2.10, an allocation of Matching Contributions [select one]

_____ shall

__X__ shall not

be made to the account of a Participant who is not employed on the [select one]

_____ Valuation Date.

__X__ last day of the Plan Year.

D.   A Participant shall be permitted to direct the investment of [select one]

_____ no part of his or her Account.

_____ his or her Elective Deferrals only.

_____ his or her Elective Deferrals and Matching Contributions.

__X__ his or her Account.

E.   If directed investments are permitted, the investment alternatives shall be [select one]

_____ selected by the Committee in its sole discretion.

__X__ such investments as the Participant may select.

If directed investments are permitted, changes in investment decisions shall be made [select one]

__X__ whenever the Participant wishes.

_____ at such times during the Plan Year as the Committee shall determine, in its sole discretion.

F.   For purposes of allocating gains and losses pursuant to Sections 10.02 and 10.03 [select one]

_____ a weighted average shall be used with reference to amounts attributable to contributions made during the Plan Year.

__X__ all contributions shall be treated as made on the last day of the Plan Year.

If amounts are held in a separate account pursuant to the provisions of Section 7.16, gains and losses

_____ shall

_____ shall not

be allocated to such amounts.

G.   Employer contributions shall be allocated to Employees [select if applicable]

__X__ who have become Disabled during the Plan Year.

__X__ who have reached Actual Retirement Date during the Plan Year.

__X__ who dies during the Plan Year.

H. Distributions on account of Hardship as defined in Section 1.37

    __X__ shall

    _____ shall not

    be permitted.

I. The Required Beginning Date of a Participant with respect to a Plan is [select one]

    _____ the April 1st of the calendar year following the calendar in which the Participant attains Age seventy and one-half (70½).

    _____ the April 1st of the calendar year following the calendar year in which the Participant attains Age seventy and one-half (70½) except that benefit distributions to a Participant (other than a 5-percent owner) with respect to benefits accrued after the later of the adoption or effective date of the amendment to the Plan must commence by the later of the April 1st of the calendar year following the calendar year in which the Participant attains Age seventy and one-half (70½) or retires.

    __X__ the later of the April 1st of the calendar year following the calendar year in which the Participant attains Age seventy and one-half (70½) or retires except that benefit distributions to a 5-percent owner must commence by the April 1st of the calendar year following the calendar year in which the Participant attains Age seventy and one-half (70½).

    In addition, you must also select one/all of the applicable choices. The third choice must be selected to the extent that there would otherwise be an elimination of a preretirement Age seventy and one-half (70½) distribution option for Employees older than those listed above.

    _____ any Participant attaining Age seventy and one-half (70½) in years after 1995 may elect by April 1st of the calendar year following the year in which the Participant attained Age seventy and one-half (70½), (or by December 31, 1997 in the case of a Participant attaining Age seventy and one-half (70½) in 1996) to defer distributions until the calendar year following the calendar year in which the Participant retires. If no such election is made the Participant will begin receiving distributions by the April 1st of the calendar year following the year in which the Participant attained Age seventy and one-half (70½) (or by December 31, 1997 in the case of a Participant attaining Age seventy and one-half (70½) in 1996).

_____ any Participant attaining Age seventy and one-half (70½) in years prior to 1997 may elect to stop distributions and recommence by the April 1st of the calendar year following the year in which the Participant retires. There is either [select one]

_____ a new annuity starting date upon recommencement, or

_____ no new annuity starting date upon recommencement.

_____ the preretirement Age seventy and one-half (70½) distribution option is only eliminated with respect to Employees who reach Age seventy and one-half (70½) in or after a calendar year that begins after the later of December 31, 1998, or the adoption date of the amendment. The preretirement Age seventy and one-half (70½) distribution option is an optional form of benefit under which benefits payable in a particular distribution form (including any modifications that may be elected after benefit commencement) commence at a time during the period that begins on or after January 1st of the calendar year in which an Employee attains Age seventy and one-half (70½) and ends April 1st of the immediately following calendar year.

Item 9: MINIMUM AND MAXIMUM CONTRIBUTIONS

A. In no event shall the Employer Contribution for the Plan Year for any Participant be in an amount less than [select one or leave blank]

$_____ [insert dollar amount].

_____% [insert percentage] of his or her Compensation for the Limitation Year which [select one]

_____ ends

_____ begins

in the Plan Year.

B. In no event shall the Employer Contribution for the Plan Year for any Participant be in an amount greater than [select one or leave blank]

$_____ [insert dollar amount].

_____% [insert percentage] of his or her Compensation for the Limitation Year which [select one]

_____ ends

_____ begins

in the Plan Year.

Item 10: VALUATION DATE

The Valuation Date shall be [check one and complete as necessary]

_____ the first day of the Plan Year.

__X__ the last day of the Plan Year.

_____ the first day of the Plan Year and the first day of the month beginning six (6) months later.

_____ the last day of the sixth (6th) month of the Plan Year and the last day of the Plan Year.

_____ the first day of each quarter of the Plan Year.

_____ the last day of each quarter of the Plan Year.

_____ daily.

_____ [insert date or series of dates - a valuation must be done at least once per year] _____.

Item 11: METHOD OF FUNDING

The Plan shall be funded as [select one]

_____ an Uninsured Plan.

___X___ a Plan funded in part with life insurance or annuity Policies.

_____ a Fully Insured Plan.

Item 12: PRERETIREMENT DEATH BENEFIT

A.   If the Plan is an Uninsured Plan, the preretirement death benefit shall be [select one]

_____ the Qualified Preretirement Survivor Annuity.

_____ the Participant's vested Accrued Benefit.

_____ the Participant's Accrued Benefit.

B.   If the Plan is a Plan funded in part with life insurance Policies the preretirement death benefit shall be [select one]

_____ the death benefit provided under any life insurance Policies issued on the Participant's life, but in no event less than the Qualified Preretirement Survivor Annuity.

___X___ the death benefit provided under any life insurance Policies issued on the Participant's life, plus the value of the Participant's Account.

C.   If the Plan is a Fully Insured Plan, the preretirement death benefit shall be [select one]

_____ the death benefit provided under any life insurance Policies issued on the Participant's life, but in no event less than the Qualified Preretirement Survivor Annuity.

_____ the death benefit provided under any life insurance Policies issued on the Participant's life, plus the cash value of any annuity Policies held in the Participant's Account.

In all cases, the Qualified Preretirement Survivor Annuity shall be paid in accordance with the provisions of Section 5.06(b) and any preretirement death benefit in excess of the value of the Qualified Preretirement Survivor Annuity shall be paid in accordance with the provisions of Section 4.07.

Item 13: *LIFE INSURANCE*

A.   If the Plan is an Insured Plan, the amount of life insurance to be purchased shall be [select one]

    _____ determined in accordance with the elections made in Item 13B.

    determined by each Participant in accordance with the elections made in Item 13C.

    _____ determined by the Committee in a nondiscriminatory manner.

B.   In the event life insurance is to be purchased pursuant to the elections made in this Item 13B, the Committee shall direct the Trustee to use [select one]

    _____% [insert percentage less than 50%] of each annual Employer contribution to purchase ordinary life insurance.

    _____% [insert percentage not in excess of 25%] of each annual Employer contribution to purchase term insurance.

    _____% [insert percentage not in excess of 25%] of each annual Employer contribution to purchase universal life insurance.

    _____% [insert percentage] of each annual Employer contribution to purchase a combination of ordinary life and term or universal life insurance in such proportion as shall be determined by the Committee, taking into account one-half (½) of the whole life premium plus the term or universal life insurance premium.

In the event the percentage of annual Employer contribution set forth above shall be insufficient to pay the premium on Policies in force on a Participant's life during the Plan Year immediately preceding the Plan Year for which the determination is being made, the Committee shall, subject to the provisions of Section 3.07 [select one]

    _____ direct the Trustee to pay such amount of the premium as is necessary from the Account of the Participant.

_____ direct the Trustee to surrender so much of the life insurance as is necessary to prevent the premium from exceeding the percentages elected in Item 13B.

_____ exercise its discretion to determine whether the premium should be paid or part of the life insurance surrendered.

In addition to amounts available for insurance under other elections in the Adoption Agreement, amounts held in a Participant's Account for at least two (2) years [select one]

__X__ shall

_____ shall not

be available for the payment of life insurance premiums.

In addition to amounts available for insurance under other elections in the Adoption Agreement, amounts held in the account of a Participant who has been such for at least five (5) years [select one]

__X__ shall

_____ shall not

be available for the payment of life insurance premiums.

C. If the Participant elects to have part of his or her Account invested in life insurance, such life insurance shall insure [select one]

_____ only the Participant's life.

__X__ the Participant's life and/or the lives of other in whom the Participant has an insurable interest and on whose life the Participant elects to purchase such insurance.

In the event the provisions of Section 3.07 shall prevent the payment of the premiums on Policies purchased in accordance with the direction of a Participant, the Committee shall direct the Trustee to surrender so much of the life insurance as is necessary to prevent the premium from exceeding the limitations set forth in Section 3.07 unless the Participant or some other person agrees to purchase such insurance from the Plan in accordance with the procedures set forth in applicable Prohibited Transaction Exemptions.

D.   [Complete if applicable] In the event a Participant is entitled on initial entry to less than $2,000 [insert amount not in excess of $2,000] of life insurance until the Participant is entitled to such amount no Policy shall be issued on the life of such Participant.

E.   [Complete if applicable] In the event a Participant is entitled as of any date to an increase in life insurance benefits that is less than $1,000 insert amount not in excess of $1,000] no life insurance Policy need be purchased until the Participant is entitled to at least the amount set forth as additional life insurance.

F.   Additional life insurance shall be purchased on the life of a Participant until the Participant [select one]

   _____ is within _____ [insert number not greater than 5]years of his or her Normal Retirement Date.

   _____ reaches his Normal Retirement Age.

   __X__ actually retires.

G.   The Committee [select one]

   _____ shall purchase key man insurance.

   __X__ shall have the right to purchase key man insurance.

   _____ shall not have the right to purchase key man insurance.

Item 14: EMPLOYEE CONTRIBUTIONS [Complete if applicable]

A.   [Not Applicable]

B.   [Not Applicable]

C.   If a voluntary contributions account is held under the Plan for a Participant, the Participant [select one if applicable]

X shall

_____ shall not

have the right to direct the investment of such account.

Item 15: VESTING

A. In any Plan Year during which the Plan is a Top-Heavy Plan, the following vesting schedule shall apply: [select one]

X Vesting in the Accrued Benefit from Employer Contributions shall be twenty (20%) percent after two (2) Years of Service, with an additional twenty (20%) percent vesting for each additional Year of Service thereafter, up to a maximum vesting in the Accrued Benefit of one hundred (100%) percent.

_____ Vesting in the Accrued Benefit from Employer Contributions shall be [complete each percentage]

_____% [insert any percentage not less than zero] after one (1) Year of Service;

_____% [not less than 20%] after two (2) Years of Service;

_____% [not less than 40%] after three (3) Years of Service;

_____% [not less than 60%] after four (4) Years of Service;

_____% [not less than 80%] after five (5) Years of Service;

100% after six (6) Years of Service.

_____ Vesting in the Accrued Benefit from Employer Contributions shall be one hundred (100%) percent after _____ [insert a number no greater than 3] Years of Service.

_____ Vesting in the Accrued Benefit from Employer Contributions shall be one hundred (100%) percent at all times. [Note: this Item must be selected if the Plan excludes Employees who have completed more than one (1) Year of Service based on a service requirement]

If the vesting schedule under the Plan shifts in or out of the above schedule for any Plan Year because of the Plan's Top-Heavy status, such shift is an amendment to the vesting schedule and the provisions of Section 12.07 of the Plan apply.

B.   In any Plan Year in which the Plan is not a Top-Heavy Plan, the following vesting schedule shall apply: [select one]

__X__ the schedule selected in Item 15A.

_____ Vesting in the Accrued Benefit from Employer Contributions shall be twenty (20%) percent after three (3) Years of Service, with an additional twenty (20%) percent vesting for each additional Year of Service thereafter, up to a maximum vesting in the Accrued Benefit of one hundred (100%) percent.

_____ Vesting in the Accrued Benefit from Employer Contributions shall be [complete each percentage]

_____% [insert any percentage not less than zero] after one (1) Year of Service;

_____% [insert any percentage not less than zero] after two (2) Years of Service;

_____% [not less than 20%] after three (3) Years of Service;

_____% [not less than 40%] after four (4) Years of Service;

_____% [not less than 60%] after five (5) Years of Service;

_____% [not less than 80%] after six (6) Years of Service;

100% after seven (7) Years of Service.

_____ Vesting in the Accrued Benefit from Employer Contributions shall be one hundred (100%) percent after _____ [insert a number no greater than 5] Years of Service.

_____ Vesting in the Accrued Benefit from Employer Contributions shall be one hundred (100%) percent at all times. [Note: this Item must be selected if the Plan excludes Employees who have completed more than one (1) Year of Service based on a service requirement]

C.   Years of Service with the Employer shall be counted to determine the non-forfeitable percentage in such Employee's Accrued Benefit from Employer Contributions based on the following elections: [select applicable exclusions]

_____ all Years of Service will be counted.

__X__ Years of Service completed before the Participant attained Age eighteen (18) shall not be included.

_____ Years of Service during a period for which the Employee made no mandatory contributions shall not be included.

__X__ Years of Service completed before the Employer maintained this Plan or a predecessor Plan shall not be included.

_____ Years of Service before January 1, 1971, unless the Employee has at least three (3) Years of Service after December 31, 1970.

_____ Years of Service before the effective date of ERISA if such Years would have been disregarded under the break in service rules of the Plan or prior plan in effect from time to time before such date. For this purpose, break in service rules are rules which result in the loss of prior vesting or benefit accruals, or deny an Employee eligibility to participate by reason of separation or failure to complete a required period of service within a specified period of time.

D.   Years of Service for purposes of determining a Participant's nonforfeitable percentage in his or her Accrued Benefit (the vesting computation period) shall be measured over [select one]

__X__ the Plan Year.

_____ the twelve (12) consecutive month periods measured from the date the Participant performs his or her first Hour of Service and each anniversary thereof.

_____ the twelve (12) consecutive month period measured from each _____ [insert month and day].

E.   [Complete if applicable] For purposes of measuring a Year of Participation or Service for accrual purposes, a Participant will be credited with a Year of Participation or Service only if he or she completes at least 1,000 [insert number not more than 1,000] Hours of Service during the accrual computation period.

[Complete if applicable] For purposes of measuring a Year of Participation or Service for vesting purposes, a Participant will be credited with a Year of Participation or Service only if he or she completes at least 1,000 [insert number not more than 1,000] Hours of Service during the vesting computation period.

Item 16: PLAN YEAR

The Plan Year shall be [select one]

_____ the twelve (12) consecutive month period which coincides with the Limitation Year.

__X__ the twelve (12) consecutive month period commencing on the Effective Date and each anniversary thereof.

_____ the twelve (12) consecutive month period commencing on _____ [insert month and day] and each anniversary thereof.

Item 17: LIMITATION YEAR

The Limitation Year shall be [select one]

__X__ the twelve (12) consecutive month period selected in Item 4D.

_____ the Plan Year.

_____ the fiscal year of the Employer.

_____ the twelve (12) consecutive month period beginning with each _____ [insert month and day].

_____ the calendar year.

Item 18: TOP-HEAVY DETERMINATIONS

A.   For purposes of establishing present value to compute the Top-Heavy Ratio, any benefit shall be discounted based on the following assumptions: [select one]

   X   the UP-84 mortality table and interest at the rate of six (6%) percent for both preretirement and post-retirement purposes.

   _____   Preretirement [complete both items; if no mortality table is used, insert "None"]

        Interest rate _____ %

        Mortality Table _____

        Other [insert assumptions] _____

Post-Retirement [complete both interest and mortality items; complete cost of living only if applicable]

        Interest rate _____ %

        Mortality Table _____

        Cost of Living _____

        Other [insert assumptions] _____

B.   For purposes of computing the Top-Heavy Ratio, the Valuation Date shall be [select one] December 31st [insert date used for computing Plan costs for minimum funding, regardless of whether a valuation is performed every year].

   _____   the Valuation Date of the defined benefit plan.

C.   Top-Heavy Minimums will be satisfied by [select one]

   X   this Plan.

   _____   another Plan.

If the Top-Heavy Minimums will be satisfied by another plan, insert the name of such other plan: _____.

D. An Employer who maintains both a defined benefit and defined contribution plan which are Top-Heavy Plans shall provide a minimum benefit or contribution in the [select one]

_____ defined benefit

_____ defined contribution

plan equal to

[if the defined benefit plan is selected]

_____% of average Compensation for the five (5) highest consecutive years after January 1, 1984, expressed as a life annuity commencing at the Participant's Normal Retirement Date, for each Plan Year after [insert date] _____ up to a maximum monthly pension of _____% [insert percentage not less than 20%] of such average Compensation.

[if the defined contribution plan is selected]

_____% of Annual Compensation for each Plan Year after [insert date] _____.

Item 19: ELECTIONS AGAINST SURVIVOR BENEFITS [check if applicable]

_____ A Participant may not make waivers concerning retirement benefits or death benefits, and may not designate a nonspouse as Beneficiary.

_____ A Participant may not waive the requirement that benefits be paid in the form of a Qualified Joint and Survivor Annuity.

_____ A Participant may not waive the requirement that a death benefit be paid in the form of a Qualified Preretirement Survivor Annuity.

_____ A married Participant may not designate a nonspouse Beneficiary as his or her primary Beneficiary.

Item 20: PARTICIPANT LOANS

Loans to Participants and their Beneficiaries [select one]

__X__ are allowed.

_____ are not allowed.

If loans are available to Participants, interest paid on such loans

__X__ shall

_____ shall not

be allocated to the Accrued Benefit of the Participant or Beneficiary borrowing the amount.

Item 21: SUSPENSION OF BENEFITS

[Not Applicable]

Item 22: BENEFIT DISTRIBUTIONS

A. A Participant who reaches his or her Normal Retirement Age but does not retire shall commence to receive his or her benefits [select one]

_____ at his or her Normal Retirement Date.

_____ at his or her Actual Retirement Date.

__X__ at any time elected by the Participant after his or her Normal Retirement Date.

Notwithstanding the election made in this Item 22A no Participant shall be required to take a distribution from the Plan prior to the later of his or her Normal Retirement Age or his or her attainment of Age sixty-two (62).

B. If benefits are not paid to a Participant who reaches his or her Normal Retirement Age but does not retire, such benefits shall be [select one]

_____ invested as part of Trust assets, with gains and losses allocated proportionately to the Participant's Account.

    X invested in the manner directed by the Participant, with the assets chosen by the Participant held in the Participant's Account.

C.   A Participant who terminates employment prior to his or her Normal Retirement Date shall be entitled to a distribution of his or her benefits [select one; the last two choices may be selected in addition to any other]

    _____ upon termination of employment.

    _____ upon the last day of the Plan Year in which termination of employment occurs.

    _____ upon termination of employment as a result of a disability as defined in Section 5.03.

    _____ upon the occurrence of a one-year Break in Service.

    _____ upon the occurrence of _____ [insert number not greater than 5] one-year Breaks in Service.

    _____ only upon the earlier of his or her death or attainment of his or her Normal Retirement Age.

    X upon the Valuation Date coincident with or next following termination of employment.

    _____ In addition, distributions can be made on the Participant's Early Retirement Date.

    X In addition, distributions can be made as a result of disability as defined in Section 5.03.

No selection made under this Item 22C shall cause benefits to be distributable later than the latest date determined under Section 4.03 of the Plan.

D.   A Spouse who is entitled to a Qualified Preretirement Survivor Annuity [select one]

    X shall

_____ shall not

be entitled to receive the Annuity in the form of a lump sum.

E.   A Participant shall be entitled to receive a distribution of his rollover account as defined in Section 5.12 [select one]

_____ at any time he or she requests.

__X__ at the same time as a distribution can be made from the Plan of all or any part of his Accrued Benefit.

F.   [Insert percentage if applicable] In lieu of a Qualified Joint and Survivor Annuity, the survivor annuity payable under the Qualified Joint and Survivor Annuity Form shall be _____% [not less than fifty (50%) percent or more than one hundred (100%) percent] of the amount of the annuity payable during the joint lives of the Participant and spouse.

G.   Distributions to a Participant in a profit sharing Plan shall be available [select applicable choices]

_____ of any amounts held in the Participant's Account for at least two (2) years.

_____ of any amounts held in the Participant's Account if the Participant has participated in the Plan for at least five (5) years.

_____ attainment of Age fifty-nine and one-half (59½).

__X__ only at the times and to the extent selected for distributions of Employer contributions in other Items in the Adoption Agreement.

Item 23: OPTIONAL FORMS

A.   Benefits shall be payable to a Participant only in one of the following forms: [complete only if the safe harbor rule of Section 5.06(b)(6) is to apply]

_____ a lump sum.

_____ a lump sum but only if the Participant is disabled as defined in Section 5.03.

_____ a lump sum but only at death.

_____ a lump sum but only at the Participant's Normal Retirement Date.

_____ a lump sum but only at the Participant's Normal Retirement Date or death.

_____ a period certain as elected by the Participant, but not in excess of _____ [insert period no greater than 20] years.

B.1. If the safe harbor rule of Section 5.06(b)(6) is not to apply, benefits payable to a Participant shall be payable in any one of the following forms, in addition to the form of a Qualified Joint and Survivor Annuity: [check all applicable forms]

_____ an annuity for the life of the Participant.

_____ an annuity for the life of the Participant, with up to _____ [select number of payments not in excess of 240] monthly payments guaranteed.

_____ a lump sum.

_____ a lump sum but only if the Participant is disabled as defined in Section 5.03.

_____ a lump sum but only at death.

_____ a lump sum but only at the Participant's Normal Retirement Date.

_____ a lump sum but only at the Participant's Normal Retirement Date or death.

_____ a lump sum to the Participant of the present value of the benefit other than the survivor annuity payable under the Qualified Joint and Survivor Annuity form, with the value of such survivor annuity payable to the spouse upon the death of the Participant.

_____ a joint and survivor annuity with spouse with _____ [insert % not more than 100%, or insert the word "any"] of the monthly pension payable to the Participant to be paid to the spouse following the death of the Participant.

_____ subject to the provisions of Section 5.06, a joint and survivor annuity with any person with _____ [insert % not more than 100%, or insert the word "any"] of the monthly pension payable to the Participant to be paid to such person on the death of the Participant.

_____ the optional form set forth in a Participant's election pursuant to section 242(b)(2) of the Tax Equity and Fiscal Responsibility Act, as set forth in Section 5.10.

__X__ all of the optional forms listed above with the lump sum payable at any time.

B.2. The optional forms of distribution above:

_____ shall

_____ shall not

reflect an amendment pursuant to Internal Revenue Regulations 1.411(d)(4) to simplify Plan administration.

B.3. In connection with certain corporate transactions (such as a merger or acquisition) or with a Participant's change of status (transfer to a subsidiary e.g.) an immediate distribution

_____ may

_____ may not

be made to such other plan at the Participant's request, even if prior to a distribution event under this Plan.

C. If benefits are payable in a lump sum under any optional form, such benefits shall be payable [select as applicable]

__X__ in any case in which the Participant so elects.

_____ only if the lump sum benefit has a value less than $_____ [insert dollar amount].

_____ only if the Participant executes an agreement not to compete with the Employer, and the conditions set forth in Section 5.07(f) have been satisfied.

D.   Benefits payable to a Participant [select one]

__X__ can only be paid in one of the optional forms set forth in Item 23A or B.

_____ can be converted to an account balance and paid in accordance with the provisions of section 401(a)(9) as they apply to distributions from an account balance.

Item 24: ROLLOVER ACCOUNTS

A.   Rollover accounts [select one]

__X__ are permitted.

_____ are not permitted.

B.   If rollover accounts are permitted, the directed investment of rollover accounts by the Participant [select one, if applicable]

__X__ is permitted.

_____ is not permitted.

C.   If rollover accounts are permitted, the Participant shall be entitled to direct the investment of [select one]

_____ no part

__X__ all

_____ [insert percentage] _____%

of his rollover account to the purchase of life insurance.

D.   If rollover accounts are permitted, and the Participant is permitted to invest any part or all of his rollover account in life insurance, the Participant may direct the purchase of life insurance [check those applicable]

   X   only on the Participant's life.

   X   on the life of the Participant jointly with another in whom the Participant has an insurable interest.

   X   on the life of any individual in whom the Participant has an insurable interest.

Item 25: LIMITATIONS ON BENEFITS

If the Employer maintains or ever maintained another qualified money purchase or profit sharing plan in which any Participant in this Plan is or was a Participant or could possibly become a Participant, the Employer adopting this Plan must complete this Item. The Employer must also complete this Item if it maintains a welfare benefit fund, as defined in section 419(e) of the Code, or an individual medical account, as defined in section 415(l)(2) of the Code, under which amounts are treated as Annual Additions with respect to any Participant in this Plan.

A.   If the Participant is covered under another qualified defined contribution Plan maintained by the Employer, other than a master or prototype plan [select one]

   _____ the provisions of Section 8.02 shall apply as if the other plan were a master or prototype plan.

   _____ [state method under which the plans will limit total Annual Additions to the Maximum Permissible Amount, and will properly reduce any excess amounts, in a manner that precludes Employer discretion]

B.   If the Participant is or has ever been a Participant in a defined benefit plan maintained by the Employer [state method which satisfied the 1.0 limitation of section 415(e) of the Code prior to the Plan Year beginning in 2000 and precludes Employer discretion]

Item 26: MISCELLANEOUS

The adopting Employer may rely on an opinion letter issued by the Internal Revenue Service as evidenced that the Plan is qualified under section 401 of the Internal Revenue Code only to the extent provided in Announcement 2001-77, 2001-30 I.R.B.

The Employer may not rely on the opinion letter in certain other circumstances or with respect to certain qualification requirements, which are specified in the opinion letter issued with respect to the plan and in Announcement 2001-77.

In order to have reliance in such circumstances or with respect to such qualification requirements, application for a determination letter must be made to Employee Plans Determinations of the Internal Revenue Service.

B. This Adoption Agreement may be used only in conjunction with The Fair, Aufsesser & FitzGerald, P.C. Defined Contribution Prototype Plan and Trust Agreement 01.

C. In the event this Adoption Agreement is improperly completed, the Plan may not be qualified under section 401(a) of the Internal Revenue Code.

D. The Sponsor will inform each adopting Employer of any amendments made to the Plan or the abandonment or discontinuance of the Plan.

E. The name, address and telephone number of the Sponsor are:

Fair, Aufsesser & FitzGerald, P.C.
110 Corporate Park Drive
White Plains, New York 10604
(914) 253-8600
(914) 253-8610 (fax)

IN WITNESS WHEREOF, the Employer and the Committee, respectively, have caused these presents to be signed by their duly authorized representatives and have caused their respective corporate seals, where required, to be hereunto affixed, as of the Effective Date.

SPECIMEN FOR *THE 401(k) ADVISOR*

Employer

BY:_____
                                            Title

SEYMOUR MONEY, Committee Member

If no separate trust agreement is signed, the Trustees should sign below.

SEYMOUR MONEY, Trustee

AMENDMENTS

The following amendments are intended to incorporate the changes required by the Economic Growth Tax Relief Reconciliation Act (EGTRRA) and final regulations relating to minimum required distributions under section 401(a)(9) of the Code. They are in the form provided by the Internal Revenue Service and are not part of the approved Defined Contribution Regional Prototype. If the Employer wishes to take advantage of the increased contribution and deduction limits permitted under EGTRRA, or the more flexible distribution provisions under the final regulations, an additional signature is required to these amendments. These amendments are intended in part as a good faith compliance with the requirements of EGTRRA and is to be construed in accordance with EGTRRA and guidance issued thereunder. These amendments shall supersede the provisions of the Plan to the extent those provisions are inconsistent with the provisions of these amendments.

The following additional provisions are adopted for this Plan and override any contradictory provision in the Plan or Adoption Agreement::

Limitations on Contributions

1. Effective date. This section shall be effective for Limitation Years beginning after December 31, 2001.

2. Maximum Annual Addition. Except to the extent permitting catch-up contributions below and section 414(v) of the Code, if applicable, the Annual

Addition that may be contributed or allocated to a Participant's Account under the Plan for any Limitation Year shall not exceed the lesser of:

(a)   Forty Thousand ($40,000) Dollars, as adjusted for increases in the cost-of-living under section 415(d) of the Code, or

(b)   One hundred (100%) percent of the Participant's Compensation, within the meaning of section 415(c)(3) of the Code, for the Limitation Year.

The Compensation limit referred to in (b) shall not apply to any contribution for medical benefits after separation from service (within the meaning of section 401(h) or section 419(A)(f)(2) of the Code) which is otherwise treated as an Annual Addition.

Increase in Compensation Limit

The Annual Compensation of each Participant taken into account in determining allocations for any Plan Year beginning after December 31, 2001, shall not exceed $200,000, as adjusted for cost-of-living increases in accordance with section 401(a)(17)(B) of the Code. Annual Compensation means Compensation during the Plan Year or such other consecutive 12-month period over which Compensation is otherwise determined under the Plan (the determination period). The cost-of-living adjustment in effect for a calendar year applies to Annual Compensation for the determination period that begins with or within such calendar year.

401(k) Plan Provisions

The following provisions shall apply to a 401(k) Plan:

1.   <u>Elective Deferrals - Contribution Limitation</u>. No Participant shall be permitted to have Elective Deferrals made under this Plan, or any other qualified plan maintained by the Employer during any taxable year, in excess of the dollar limitation contained in section 402(g) of the Code in effect for such taxable years, except to the extent permitted under the section of this amendment permitting catch-up contributions and section 414(v) of the Code, if applicable.

2.   <u>Maximum Salary Reduction Contributions</u>

Except to the extent permitted under the section of this amendment permitting catch-up contributions and section 414(v) of the Code, if applicable, the maximum salary reduction contribution that can be made to this Plan is the amount determined under section 408(p)(2)(A)(ii) of the Code for the calendar year.

3.   Multiple Use Test. The multiple use test described in Section 1.401(m)-2 of the Income Tax Regulations shall not apply for Plan Years beginning after December 31, 2001.

4.   Global search 402(g). No Participant shall be permitted to have Elective Deferrals made under this Plan, or any other qualified plan maintained by the Employer during any taxable year, in excess of the dollar limitation contained in section 402(g) of the Code in effect for such taxable year, except to the extent of any catch-up contributions under section 414(v) of the Code permitted under the Plan.

5.   Top-Heavy Exception. The Top-Heavy requirements of section 416 of the Code shall not apply in any year beginning after December 31, 2001, in which the Plan consists solely of a cash or deferred arrangement which meets the requirements of section 401(k)(12) of the Code and matching contributions with respect to which the requirements of section 401(m)(11) of the Code are met.

6.   Catch-Up Contributions. If the Employer advises its Employees in writing that catch-up contributions are permitted all Employees who are eligible to make elective deferrals under this Plan and who have attained Age fifty (50) before the close of the Plan Year shall be eligible to make catch-up contributions in accordance with, and subject to the limitations of, section 414(v) of the Code. Such catch-up contributions shall not be taken into account for purposes of the provisions of the Plan implementing the required limitations of sections 402(g) and 415 of the Code. The Plan shall not be treated as failing to satisfy the provisions of the Plan implementing the requirements of section 401(k)(3), 401(k)(11), 401(k)(12), 410(b), or 416 of the Code, as applicable, by reason of the making of such catch-up contributions.

7.   Prohibition against additional deferrals following Hardship distribution. A Participant who receives a distribution of Elective Deferrals on account of Hardship shall be prohibited from making Elective Deferrals and Employee Contributions under this and all other plans of the Employer for 6 months after receipt of the distribution.

8.   New distributable event. A Participant's Elective Deferrals, Qualified Nonelective Contributions, Qualified Matching Contributions, and earnings attributable to these contributions shall be distributed on account of the Participant's severance from employment. However, such a distribution shall be subject to the other provisions of the Plan regarding distributions, other than provisions that require a separation from service before such amounts may be distributed.

Rollovers

1.   <u>Modification of definition of eligible retirement</u> plan. If a Participant is permitted under the terms of the Plan to roll funds to this Plan from another plan qualified under section 401(a) of the Code, the Participant shall also be permitted to roll funds to this Plan from a plan described in section 403(b) of the Code, a plan described under section 457(b) of the Code if otherwise permitted under the law, and any individual retirement account described in section 408 of the Code if otherwise permitted under the law. If Participant loans are permitted, the rollover account shall be considered part of the Participant's Accrued Benefit but solely for the purpose of such loans.

2.   <u>Modification of definition of eligible rollover distribution to exclude hardship distributions</u>. For purposes of the direct rollover provisions of the plan, any amount that is distributed on account of hardship shall not be an eligible rollover distribution and the distributee may not elect to have any portion of such a distribution paid directly to an eligible retirement plan.

3.   <u>Modification of definition of eligible rollover distribution to include after-tax Employee contributions</u>. For purposes of the direct rollover provisions in subsection (a) of the Plan, a portion of a distribution shall not fail to be an eligible rollover distribution merely because the portion consists of after-tax Employee contributions which are not includible in gross income. However, such portion may be transferred only to an individual retirement account or annuity described in section 408(a) or (b) of the Code, or to a qualified defined contribution plan described in section 401(a) or 403(a) of the Code that agrees to separately account for amounts so transferred, including separately accounting for the portion of such distribution which is includible in gross income and the portion of such distribution which is not so includible.

4. <u>Rollovers disregarded in determining value of account balance for involuntary distributions</u>. The value of a Participant's nonforfeitable Accrued Benefit shall be determined without regard to that portion of the Accrued Benefit that is attributable to rollover contributions (and earnings allocable thereto) within the meaning of Sections 402(c), 403(a)(4), 403(b)(8), 408(d)(3)(A)(ii), and 457(e)(16) of the Code. If the value of the Participant's nonforfeitable account balance as so determined is $5,000 or less, the Plan shall, at such times as a distribution would otherwise be permitted, immediately distribute the Participant's entire nonforfeitable account balance.

Loans

If the Plan document permits loans, commencing January 1, 2002, loans may be made to self-employed individuals and stockholders of S Corporations.

Top-Heavy Provisions

1. <u>Determination of Top-Heavy Status</u>. Key Employee means any Employee or former Employee (including any deceased Employee) who at any time during the Plan Year that includes the determination date was an officer of the Employer having annual compensation greater than $130,000 (as adjusted under Section 416(i)(1) of the Code for Plan Years beginning after December 31, 2001), a 5% owner of the Employer, or a 1% owner of the Employer having Annual Compensation of more than $150,000. For this purpose, Annual Compensation means Compensation within the meaning of Section 415(c)(3) of the Code. The determination of who is a Key Employee will be made in accordance with Section 416(i)(1) of the Code and the applicable regulations and other guidelines of general applicability issued thereunder.

2. <u>Distributions during year ending on the determination date</u>. The present values of Accrued Benefits and the amounts of account balances of an Employee as of the determination date shall be increased by the distributions made with respect to the Employee under the Plan and any plan aggregated with the Plan under Section 416(g)(2) of the Code during the one year period ending on the determination date. The preceding sentence shall also apply to distributions under a terminated Plan which, had it not been terminated, would have been aggregated with the Plan under Section 416(g)(2(A)(i) of the Code. In the case of a distribution made for a reason

other than separation from service, death, or disability, this provision shall be applied by substituting A5-year period for A1-year period.

3. <u>Employees not performing services during year ending on the determination date</u>. The Accrued Benefits and accounts of any individual who has not performed services for the Employer during the one year period ending on the determination date shall not be taken into account.

4. <u>Top-Heavy Minimum Contribution Requirement</u>. Elective Deferrals may not be taken into account for the purpose of satisfying the minimum Top-Heavy contribution requirement. Employer Matching Contributions shall be taken into account for purposes of satisfying the minimum contribution requirements of section 416(c)(2) of the Code and the Plan. The preceding sentence shall apply with respect to Matching Contributions under the Plan or, if the Plan provides that the minimum contribution requirement shall be met in another plan, such other plan. Employer Matching Contributions that are used to satisfy the minimum contribution requirements shall be treated as Matching Contributions for purposes of the actual contribution percentage test and other requirements of Section 401(m) of the Code.

5. <u>Contributions under the plans</u>. The Employer may provide in the Adoption Agreement that the minimum benefit requirement shall be met in another Plan (including another plan that consists solely of a cash or deferred arrangement which meets the requirements of section 401(k)(12) of the Code and Matching Contributions with respect to which the requirements of section 401(m)(11) of the Code are met).

Minimum Distribution Requirements

Section 1. <u>General Rules</u>.

1.1 <u>Effective Date</u>. The provisions of this amendment will apply for purposes of determining required minimum distributions for calendar years beginning with the 2002 calendar year.

1.2 <u>Coordination with Minimum Distribution Requirements Previously in Effect</u>. Required minimum distributions for 2002 under this amendment will be determined as follows:

(a) If the total amount of 2002 required minimum distributions under the Plan made to the distributee prior to the effective date of this amendment equals or exceeds the required minimum distributions determined under this amendment, then no additional distributions will be required to be made for 2002 on or after such date to the distributee.

(b) If the total amount of 2002 required minimum distributions under the plan made to the distributee prior to the effective date of this amendment is less than the amount determined under this amendment, then required minimum distributions for 2002 on and after such date will be determined so that the total amount of required minimum distributions for 2002 made to the distributee will be the amount determined under this amendment.

1.3 Precedence. The requirements of this amendment will take precedence over any inconsistent provisions of the Plan.

1.4 Requirements of Treasury Regulations Incorporated. All distributions required under this amendment will be determined and made in accordance with the Treasury regulations under section 401(a)(9) of the Code.

1.5 TEFRA Section 242(b)(2) Elections. Notwithstanding the other provisions of this amendment, distributions may be made under a designation made before January 1, 1984, in accordance with section 242(b)(2) of the Tax Equity and Fiscal Responsibility Act (TEFRA) and the provisions of the plan that relate to section 242(b)(2) of TEFRA.

Section 2. Time and Manner of Distribution.

2.1 Required Beginning Date. The Participant's entire interest will be distributed, or begin to be distributed, to the Participant no later than the Participant's Required Beginning Date.

2.2 Death of Participant Before Distributions Begin. If the Participant dies before distributions begin, the Participant's entire interest will be distributed, or begin to be distributed, no later than as follows:

(a) If the Participant's surviving spouse is the Participant's sole Designated Beneficiary, then, except as provided in the Adoption Agreement, distributions to the surviving spouse will begin by December 31 of the calendar year immediately following the calendar year in which the Participant died, or by December 31 of the calendar year in which the Participant would have attained age 70½, if later.

(b) If the Participant's surviving spouse is not the Participant's sole Designated Beneficiary, then, except as provided in the Adoption Agreement, distributions to the Designated Beneficiary will begin by December 31 of the calendar year immediately following the calendar year in which the Participant died.

(c) If there is no Designated Beneficiary as of September 30 of the year following the year of the Participant's death, the Participant's entire interest will be distributed by December 31 of the calendar year containing the fifth anniversary of the Participant's death.

(d) If the Participant's surviving spouse is the Participant's sole Designated Beneficiary and the surviving spouse dies after the Participant but before distributions to the surviving spouse begin, this section 2.2, other than section 2.2(a), will apply as if the surviving spouse were the Participant.

For purposes of this section 2.2 and section 4, unless section 2.2(d) applies, distributions are considered to begin on the Participant's Required Beginning Date. If section 2.2(d) applies, distributions are considered to begin on the date distributions are required to begin to the surviving spouse under section 2.2(a). If distributions under an annuity purchased from an insurance company irrevocably commence to the Participant before the Participant's Required Beginning Date (or to the Participant's surviving spouse before the date distributions are required to begin to the surviving spouse under section 2.2(a)), the date distributions are considered to begin is the date distributions actually commence.

2.3 <u>Forms of Distribution</u>. Unless the participant's interest is distributed in the form of an annuity purchased from an insurance company or in a single sum on or before the Required Beginning Date, as of the first distribution calendar year distributions will be made in accordance with sections 3 and 4 of this amendment. If the Participant's interest is distributed in the form of an annuity purchased from an insurance company, distributions thereunder will be made in accordance with the requirements of section 401(a)(9) of the Code and the Treasury regulations.

Section 3. <u>Required Minimum Distributions During Participant's Lifetime</u>.

3.1 <u>Amount of Required Minimum Distribution For Each Distribution Calendar Year</u>. During the Participant's lifetime, the minimum amount that will be distributed for each distribution calendar year is the lesser of:

(a) the quotient obtained by dividing the Participant's account balance by the distribution period in the Uniform Lifetime Table set forth in section 1.401(a)(9)-9 of the Treasury regulations, using the participant's age as of the participant's birthday in the distribution calendar year; or

(b) if the Participant's sole Designated Beneficiary for the distribution calendar year is the Participant's spouse, the quotient obtained by dividing the Participant's account balance by the number in the Joint and Last Survivor Table set forth in section 1.401(a)(9)-9 of the Treasury regulations, using the Participant's and spouse's attained ages as of the Participant's and spouse's birthdays in the distribution calendar year.

3.2 <u>Lifetime Required Minimum Distributions Continue Through Year of Participant's Death</u>. Required minimum distributions will be determined under this section 3 beginning with the first distribution calendar year and up to and including the distribution calendar year that includes the Participant's date of death.

Section 4. <u>Required Minimum Distributions After Participant's Death</u>.

4.1 <u>Death On or After Date Distributions Begin</u>.

(a) <u>Participant Survived by Designated Beneficiary</u>. If the Participant dies on or after the date distributions begin and there is a Designated Beneficiary, the minimum amount that will be distributed for each distribution calendar year after the year of the Participant's death is the quotient obtained by dividing the Participant's account balance by the longer of the remaining life expectancy of the Participant or the remaining life expectancy of the Participant's Designated Beneficiary, determined as follows:

(i) The Participant's remaining life expectancy is calculated using the age of the Participant in the year of death, reduced by one for each subsequent year.

(ii) If the Participant's surviving spouse is the Participant's sole Designated Beneficiary, the remaining life expectancy of the surviving spouse is calculated for each distribution calendar year after the year of the Participant's death using the surviving spouse's age as of the spouse's birthday in that year. For distribution calendar years after the year of the surviving spouse's death, the remaining life expectancy of the surviving spouse is calculated using the age of the surviving spouse as of the spouse's birthday in the calendar year of the spouse's death, reduced by one for each subsequent calendar year.

(iii) If the Participant's surviving spouse is not the Participant's sole Designated Beneficiary, the Designated Beneficiary's remaining life expectancy is calculated using the age of the Beneficiary in the year following the year of the Participant's death, reduced by one for each subsequent year.

(b) <u>No Designated Beneficiary</u>. If the Participant dies on or after the date distributions begin and there is no Designated Beneficiary as of September 30 of the year after the year of the Participant's death, the minimum amount that will be distributed for each distribution calendar year after the year of the Participant's death is the quotient obtained by dividing the Participant's account balance by the Participant's remaining life expectancy calculated using the age of the Participant in the year of death, reduced by one for each subsequent year.

4.2 <u>Death Before Date Distributions Begin</u>.

(a) <u>Participant Survived by Designated Beneficiary</u>. Except as provided in the Adoption Agreement, if the Participant dies before the date distributions begin and there is a Designated Beneficiary, the minimum amount that will be distributed for each distribution calendar year after the year of the Participant's death is the quotient obtained by dividing the Participant's account balance by the remaining life expectancy of the Participant's Designated Beneficiary, determined as provided in section 4.1.

(b) <u>No Designated Beneficiary</u>. If the Participant dies before the date distributions begin and there is no Designated Beneficiary as of

September 30 of the year following the year of the Participant's death, distribution of the Participant's entire interest will be completed by December 31 of the calendar year containing the fifth anniversary of the Participant's death.

(c) <u>Death of Surviving Spouse Before Distributions to Surviving Spouse Are Required to Begin</u>. If the Participant dies before the date distributions begin, the Participant's surviving spouse is the Participant's sole Designated Beneficiary, and the surviving spouse dies before distributions are required to begin to the surviving spouse under section 2.2(a), this section 4.2 will apply as if the surviving spouse were the Participant.

Section 5. <u>Definitions</u>.

5.1   <u>Designated Beneficiary</u>. The individual who is designated as the Beneficiary under the Plan and is the Designated Beneficiary under section 401(a)(9) of the Internal Revenue Code and section 1.401(a)(9)-1, Q&A-4, of the Treasury regulations.

5.2   <u>Distribution calendar year</u>. A calendar year for which a minimum distribution is required. For distributions beginning before the Participant's death, the first distribution calendar year is the calendar year immediately preceding the calendar year which contains the Participant's Required Beginning Date. For distributions beginning after the Participant's death, the first distribution calendar year is the calendar year in which distributions are required to begin under section 2.2. The required minimum distribution for the Participant's first distribution calendar year will be made on or before the Participant's Required Beginning Date. The required minimum distribution for other distribution calendar years, including the required minimum distribution for the distribution calendar year in which the Participant's Required Beginning Date occurs, will be made on or before December 31 of that distribution calendar year.

5.3   <u>Life expectancy</u>. Life expectancy as computed by use of the Single Life Table in section 1.401(a)(9)-9 of the Treasury regulations.

5.4   <u>Participant's account balance</u>. The account balance as of the last valuation date in the calendar year immediately preceding the distribution calendar year (valuation calendar year) increased by the amount of any contributions made and allocated or forfeitures allocated to the account balance as of dates in the valuation calendar year after the valuation date and decreased by distributions made in the valuation calendar year after the valuation date. The account balance for the valuation calendar year includes any amounts rolled over or transferred to the plan either in the valuation calendar year or in the distribution calendar year if distributed or transferred in the valuation calendar year.

5.5 Required beginning date. The date specified in the Adoption Agreement.

Section 6. Elections with reference to 5-Year Rule.

6.1 Election by Participant or Beneficiary to Apply 5-Year Rule. Participants or Beneficiaries may elect on an individual basis whether the 5-year rule or the life expectancy rule in sections 2.2 and 5 applies to distributions after the death of a Participant who has a Designated Beneficiary. The election must be made no later than the earlier of September 30 of the calendar year in which distribution would be required to begin under section 2.2 or by September 30 of the calendar year which contains the fifth anniversary of the Participant's (or, if applicable, surviving spouse's) death. If neither the Participant nor Beneficiary makes an election under this paragraph, distributions will be made in accordance with sections 2.2 and 5 and, if applicable, the elections in section 2 above.

6.2 Election by Designated Beneficiary to Revoke 5-Year Rule. A Designated Beneficiary who is receiving payments under the 5-year rule may make a new election at any time until December 31, 2003 to receive payments under the life expectancy rule, provided that all amounts that would have been required to be distributed under the life expectancy rule for all distribution calendar years before 2004 are distributed by the earlier of December 31, 2003 or the end of the 5-year period.

The foregoing amendments are hereby adopted as part of the Plan to which they are attached.

———————————————————————
President or Owner of EMPLOYER

Index